The Gospel of Kink

A Modern Guide To Asking For What You Want And Getting What You Ask For

First Edition

Richard Wagner, Ph.D., ACS

ISBN: 978-1-61098-364-8
Ebook ISBN: 978-1-61098-365-5

Published by

The Nazca Plains Corporation ®
4640 Paradise Rd, Suite 141
Las Vegas, NV 89109-8000

Cover Image, Josef Mohyla
Author's Photo, Michael Henry
Art Direction, Blake Stephens

The Gospel of Kink

A Modern Guide To Asking For What You Want And Getting What You Ask For

First Edition

Published by The Nazca Plains Corporation
Las Vegas, Nevada
2013

Acknowledgements

I want to thank Steven Webb and Muffin Vandalya for helping me edit and proofread the book.

I am deeply grateful for the generosity of my friends, colleagues and mentors—Samantha, Lance Navarro, Byrdie, Jack Slash, and Kristen Knapick, MA, LMHCA—who volunteered their time, effort, and expertise as the panelists for this workshop-in-a-book. You will find more about them in the *About The Contributors* section at the end of the book.

Table of Contents

Foreword

I like to be a provocative. But that's not why I chose *The Gospel of Kink* as this book's title. Rather, I want to make a declaration and I want the declaration to be received as good news.

Anyone with a lick of religious upbringing, at least in the Christian tradition, will know that the word gospel means good news or glad tidings. This book is the culmination of thirty-plus years of preaching the good news of the sex-positive and kink-aware movements, especially as it applies to those of us on the sexual fringe.

Of course, the word "gospel" also suggests singular and exclusive. However, my use of this word has nothing to do with being carved in stone, or being the last word, or worse, the *only* word. The vibrancy of the kink community is, after all, dependent on its diversity.

In addition, I've never particularly liked the word "lifestyle" as it relates to the world of sexual minorities. I think the term is old-fashioned and outdated. I also think it's a misnomer and, apparently, a lot of other people in the kink and BDSM scene feel the same way. For many years, I used the term "subculture" instead of "lifestyle" when referring to groups of people on the sexual fringe. It seemed to me more appropriate as well as more accurate. But in the last couple of years, my thinking about this has evolved further. I had to ask myself, "Why did I need to preface 'culture' with the unnecessary modifier 'sub?'" You'll pardon the pun, but there's nothing sub about our culture.

So in an effort to help all of us change our vocabulary, I'm using the word "culture" to replace "lifestyle" throughout the book. For clarity's sake, I also use the term "alt culture" as a way of differentiating it from the popular or dominant culture.

Making a conspicuous change in vocabulary is revolutionary. This is particularly so when the shift comes as a result of a person reconceptionalizing who they are. It's also obvious that our personal evolution always has a ripple effect on those around us. So much so that, in the end, a simple statement about who we are, one that is informed by our thoughtful self-reflection, becomes a gospel declaration. And that, to my mind, is truly provocative.

"I believe that sex is a beautiful thing between two people. Between five, it's fantastic."

Woody Allen

Introduction

Getting Started

We'd be willing to guess that you've tried other, more mainstream relationship books, seminars and workshops before hooking up with us. That's great! It tells us that you are searching for answers. And as the old saying goes, "Seek and ye shall find."

The problem with the mainstream, to put it bluntly, is we don't fit in. Despite our efforts to translate the good advice we may get from conventional sources, the advice doesn't always fit. Buying off the rack, when you know that you really need something tailored, simply won't do.

We kinksters need something radically different. We need a way to access information, explore our feelings, and learn from others in our alt culture. We need a safe and secure place to air our concerns without fearing that we will be judged for how we choose to live our lives or for who we choose to live our lives with.

What you will find here is a chance to confront your relationship concerns in a truly adventurous way. We invite you to jump into the interactive environment we provide and become a member of our on-the-page workshop.

Each of the following chapters will involve you in this process. You'll get to know and identify with the issues and concerns of the other workshop participants. You'll be able to involve yourself fully in all the discussions and exercises.

You'll also be challenged by a panel of skilled practitioners who will offer you valuable information on timely issues such as communication, power exchange, polyamory, jealousy, sex and intimacy, relationship concerns, and conflict resolution.

You'll receive the encouragement you need to design your own practical solutions to the unique alt-cultural issues you face. We will help you develop a strategy for successfully navigating the pitfalls that can plague those of us on the sexual fringe.

And the best part is you can do it all at your own pace. You won't have to tear through your closet looking for something to wear, fight traffic, search for a parking space, or rush to get here on time. You can just "show up" by getting comfortable wherever you are.

Let's make one thing clear from the start. There's no single way to live a happy, healthy, and integrated kinky and alt culture life. However, there are some things you might want to consider if that is your goal.

- First, just because we're different doesn't make us second-class.
- While it may be easy to accept our kinky identity in the abstract, it's often more difficult to manage the specifics of our unique alt-culture expression. *Why can't I connect with people who understand me? Why do my relationships fail, even though I work hard at them? Why is it so difficult for me to express myself to my partners?* These are some of the most difficult questions kinky and alt-culture people ask themselves.
- Living a healthy kinky and alt-culture life begins the moment we accept our eroticism as part of our core identities. We've had to integrate other aspects of who we are into our daily lives including our gender, racial background, and cultural heritage, to name a few. Why not our sexual proclivities and eroticism?
- Integrating our kinky eroticism into our lives and celebrating it can lead to a deep emotional intensity. It's possible to harness this intensity and make this the culminating stage of our personal growth.

This workbook will provide you the support you need to begin the process of creating and living healthy and life-affirming kinky, BDSM, and alt-culture relationships.

Personal Intake Form

Let's begin by taking stock of your current situation. This will give you a baseline from which to evaluate your progress throughout the program.

Some Things About You

Name:

____

Nickname or scene name:

____

Date of birth:

____

I was born and raised:

____

I currently live:

____

Religious background:

____

Current religious practice if any:

____

List five significant events in your life:

1. ______________________________
2. ______________________________
3. ______________________________
4. ______________________________
5. ______________________________

Interests, hobbies, pastimes:

____

____

____

Your Current Situation

My alt-culture life consists of:

____

____

____

My kinks and fetishes are:

____

____

____

My current support system (partner, spouse, M/s, D/s, family, tribe, friends, support groups) involves:

____

____

____

Personal Growth Goals

List three accomplishments you wish to accomplish during this workshop:

1. ______________________________
2. ______________________________
3. ______________________________

List three areas you need the most help with:

1. ______________________________
2. ______________________________
3. ______________________________

Your Fellow Participants

Now that you've completed your intake form, I'd like to offer you a sneak preview of the ten other people who will be joining you in this group. You'll have plenty of opportunity to get to know them once we get started, but until you get better acquainted, these thumbnail sketches will serve as a handy reference.

Here's a tip: You may want to bookmark this page so that you can return to this section if, at first, you find all these personalities a bit confusing.

....

Stan, 52, is single and describes himself as "your average white guy." His marriage of 26 years ended in divorce three years ago. He has always been interested in the D/s culture, but his wife would have none of it. He now regrets that he let his marriage sink to the lowest common denominator. He says, "If the truth be told, the disparity in sexual interests between me and my wife was the main reason our marriage ended."

Now that he is on his own, he says he intends to make up for lost time. Unfortunately, almost everything he thinks he knows of the D/s culture he picked up watching porn. These sexually explicit visuals have been driving his fantasies since long before the breakup of his marriage. He is eager to connect with and set up a relationship with a dominant woman, but he reeks of desperation. He also has no discernable dating skills and he often reverts to the only relationship model he knows—monogamous, heterosexual, and vanilla. He begrudgingly admits that this is not serving him very well.

Stan is successful both financially and professionally, and because of this he remains closeted about his sexual interests. This prevents him from fully immersing himself in the culture, even though he would like to. He's paranoid about being "outed" or worse.

Over the past year and a half, he has responded to a number of sex ads he saw in the back of an alternative weekly newspaper. Swallowing his pride, he actually connected with two of the pro-Dommes who placed a couple of those ads. While the these experiences were titillating, they were ultimately unfulfilling. They left him feeling anxious. He now believes that time is running out for him and he is frustrated by his lack of success in connecting with the woman of his dreams. He does not want to rely on these professional connections.

He saw a flier for this workshop at a meet-and-greet at The Wet Spot, the Center for Sex Positive Culture here in Seattle. He knows he needs to hone his communication skills, but he was put off when he discovered that the workshop was open to sexual minorities. He is uncomfortable being around those he refers to as "the gays."

....

Gretchen, 44, and **Eddie**, 48, have been happily married for seventeen years. This is the second marriage for both of them. Both claim they made the same fatal mistakes in their first marriages. Gretchen speaks for them both: "We married way too young and then we tried to conform to the sexual and relationship mores of our parents' generation. It was a disaster."

Theirs is a blended family. Gretchen had two kids and Eddie had one when they met, and then they had one daughter together. They successfully raised their four kids and now that their nest is empty, they've decided to live openly as a consensual M/s couple. Eddie is the Master, Gretchen is the slave. Happily, all their kids love and accept them for who they are.

They have a fair amount of experience with BDSM play and M/s relationships. However, in the past, their play was restricted to stolen opportunities when their kids were out of the house. Now Eddie is outfitting their basement as a home dungeon/play space.

Now that they are less restricted in their lives and sexual expression they don't want to continue dabbling around the edges. Both insist that they want to revitalize their M/s relationship and make it formal. Gretchen looks forward to being collared by Eddie and she wants this to happen in a ceremony attended by their kids and some of their close alt-culture friends.

But there is trouble in paradise. Eddie has been talking about expanding their "family" to include another female submissive. This doesn't sit well with

Gretchen. She has jealousy issues and she knows it. She's never been comfortable with even watching Eddie play with someone else, so the prospect of a live-in sub and the possibility of this turning into a polyamorous relationship shakes Gretchen to her foundation.

Gretchen says, "However this plays itself out, I want to jettison these feelings of inadequacy. I want to make my life decisions from a position of strength, not weakness. Just because I'm a slave doesn't mean I'm a doormat."

....

Sofie is 31. She is bisexual and poly to the bone. She also has what she refers to as a "wickedly kinky streak."

Her primary relationship is with Emma, who is ten years her senior. Emma self-identifies as a lesbian. They've been together for six years.

Sofie's other lover is Caleb, a Parisian-born straight guy who is two years younger than she is. Their relationship has been going hot and heavy for just over a year. Sofie doesn't live with either of her partners. This is "both a blessing and a curse," as she describes it.

Sofie and Emma are very close, but she confides that Emma can be, and often is, very territorial toward her. Emma is not all that pleased with Sofie's relationship with Caleb. "Emma and I have hashed this out a dozen times at least. The issue settles for a while till it raises its ugly head once again. We nearly broke up over this when I first started dating Caleb."

Sofie's relationship with Caleb, on the other hand, is much more casual. "Caleb is the consummate 'bad boy' and I totally get off on that. The sex thing is amazing! But I don't let myself get too close to him. Ya see, I have these 'issues' with men. I was sexually abused by a family member when I was a kid, and it left a scar a mile wide."

Sofie says that Caleb is often confused by her reluctance to deepen their involvement. He thinks the sexual connection they have is a really good indication that they should go deeper. Sofie is not so sure.

One thing is certain, Sofie readily admits that she's not as adept as she would like to be at negotiating boundaries with either of her partners. She says, "Not everyone has been open and honest, and that includes me. Each of us has our own deep-seated trust issues."

She also wants to exercise her wickedly kinky streak. She's toying with the idea of initiating a D/s relationship with Caleb. But she knows that's not possible till her (their) trust issues are addressed and resolved.

Sofie decided to attend the workshop alone, without either of her partners.

....

Mark, 36, and his husband **Willie**, 38, have been together eight years. Just as soon as Washington State permitted gay marriage, the guys made honest men of one another by getting hitched at Mark's parents' palatial estate on Whidbey Island.

Despite the fact that both Mark and Willie are successful professionals now, money issues contaminate their relationship. Willie didn't come from money like Mark did; he grew up in poverty in the Bronx. The whole discretionary income thing is a relatively new concept for him. This colors how Willie deals with money and it often puts him at odds with Mark, who thinks money grows on trees. Willie says, "Nothing can tear at a relationship like arguing about money. We hate it when it happens, but it seems to happen more and more frequently now than when we first met. I don't know, maybe it's a sign of more deep-seated issues."

Willie opposed having their wedding at Mark's parents' place because he's never been comfortable there or with them. For the longest time he thought Mark's parents didn't like him because he's black. Mark had to correct him: "It's not your color they object to; they still can't wrap their head around the fact that their son is a fag and you're my man."

Mark says, "Sex has always been great between us." Willie nods in agreement. "We met at a BDSM sex club and we've been going strong ever since."

But then Willie adds, "Yeah, that is until it comes to who's gonna fuck who, or who's gonna top who."

"When that happens," Mark continues with a laugh, "we simply go out and find ourselves a willing bottom or sub to satisfy us both."

Despite their intense sex connection, or maybe because of it, the guys wonder at the depth of their emotional relationship. Willie speaks for them both: "I mean, honestly, how connected are we if we can't, from time to time, negotiate who will bottom or sub for whom?"

....

Blake, 33, and **Alicia,** 26, met at a play party hosted by a mutual friend last year and have been playing together for the last six months. "We're like total newbies to the scene," Alicia confides.

Blake hastens to add, "Yeah, but we're doing lots of hands-on classes and demos. There's just so much to learn and we love learning together. The community is so vast and varied and most of the people we meet are eager to share what they know."

"Yeah, we look forward to giving back when it's our turn to mentor," adds Alicia.

When asked about the roles they take in their power exchange, Alicia and Blake say they are still figuring that out. "I'm generally the top," says Blake, "but I'm not sure that's not just by default, me being the guy and all. Personally, I think Alicia would be even better in that role than I am."

"It's true," Alicia interjects, "I think I'm better suited to being a top, but I also want to learn to be a top from the bottom. Does that make sense?"

Alicia and Blake aren't a "couple" in the traditional sense of that word. Each has always had permission from the other to play around with whomever they'd like. Apparently, this arrangement works out fine just as long as it's never tested. "I totally freaked out one night when Alicia topped this other dude at a play party we were at," Blake confesses.

Alicia quickly adds, "He was pissed off for days afterward. I simply didn't get it. It's not like I fucked the guy, we were just playing around with a flogger and before ya know it, I was using it on him. It was like totally innocent."

The confrontation that followed this incident revealed that Blake had kept up a sexual connection with a former girlfriend even though he told Alicia that the relationship was over. "See this is just bullshit! Why the fuck did he get all bent out of shape about me when he was doing worse?"

"I admit, that was fucked up, but I couldn't help myself," adds Blake.

The upside of the relationship confrontation is that it led Alicia and Blake to this workshop. Initially, they were going to see a mainstream relationship counselor for help, but they were afraid the therapist wouldn't understand or approve of their open relationship and BDSM life. Alicia put it this way: "I don't want anyone getting the wrong impression; being kinky isn't our problem. Being honest and open with one another is!"

....

Seiko is 29. She is the only daughter of a Japanese couple who emigrated to the US in 1975. She is as smart as a whip; she has her Ph.D. in International Affairs from Columbia University. But she's learned to dumb herself down just to fit in.

She's away from family for the first time and now lives in Bellevue, Washington. The cultural shock from East Coast to West has her reeling. "The move really messed with my head. Jeez, everything is so different here. You'd think I had moved to a different planet."

The move away from her very traditional Japanese family and East Coast friends has been a double-edged sword for Seiko. She misses the comfort of the familiar, but she realizes that the comfortable can also be stifling. Take, for example, the crush she's developed on her roommate, Xiang.

Xiang is a grad student at the University of Washington. And despite being raised in a very traditional Chinese family, Xiang is a total freak now. "I've never had a crush on a girl before," confesses Seiko. "I don't even know where this is coming from. Maybe it's because Xiang has set herself free. Maybe that's why I find her so attractive."

But actually, there's more to this infatuation than just Xiang's freedom and freakiness. Seiko is in love. She can barely say the words aloud, but when pushed on the subject, she relents. "Xiang introduced me to the scene and now I'm drawn to it and her. It's a way for me to leave everything associated with my traditional upbringing behind." But these uncharted waters are scary, and not just emotionally, because both Xiang and Seiko continue to date men.

In the scene, Seiko refuses to bottom or sub. "I'm pretty certain this is an overreaction to how Asian women are perceived in the dominant culture. I won't go there, not even in play." Xiang, on the other hand, thinks Seiko's reasoning is fucked up. She's not one for reserving her opinion and when she challenges

Seiko, there are fireworks. "Bottoms and subs aren't weak," Xiang insists. "Do you think I'm weak or subservient like some old Chinese lady because I'm a switch? You need to get over yourself, bitch!"

Seiko hates to be challenged like this by Xiang. But it also makes her want Xiang more. "I'm like going all lezzy over this. What's wrong with me? I'm so confused."

This untenable situation with Xiang is what brings Seiko to the workshop. She's wise enough to know that she needs help "pulling her head out of her ass," as Xiang would say. However, she didn't tell Xiang that she is doing this workshop. "I don't know, am I trying to deceive her, or am I just trying to have some of my own space?"

....

Brodie is 28. He was born in Glasgow but moved with his parents to the US when he was 15. He retains much of his Scottish brogue. His ruddy good looks, shock of unruly red hair, 6'3" rugby build, and killer smile make for an intoxicating combination. "I don't know, I've always been successful with the chicks. Dudes come on to me all the time too. I guess I'm just lucky."

Despite being blessed with good looks and abundant charm, Brodie has a string of disastrous affairs in his recent past. He's concerned about his reputation. Word is getting out that he is a cad. He quickly comes to his own defense, "It's not totally my fault. Things start out just fine, but then they rapidly spiral out of control. Women see what they want to see in me and when I don't turn out to be that person, everything goes belly-up."

Brodie has been kinky since he was a kid. He recalls tying up his action figures as early as age five or six. He's tried to buckle down and do the vanilla thing with any number of the women he's dated, but his true nature always gets the better of him. "I really try to be upfront with them from the start. I tell them I'm kinky. But I think they figure they can break me of this 'bad' habit. There's just no way. I swear, I'll never do vanilla again!"

Brodie now has a few years of experience in the BDSM scene and he aspires to become a Master. However, his outward appearance and bravado hide a lack of confidence. He knows he has to get a handle on this, or he'll never be the Master he wants to be. "The last thing I want to do is be one of those play-acting 'Masters' that you see in the scene all the time. I'll go back to being vanilla before I become a poser or dilettante. It's either the real thing or nothing!"

When pressed about his confidence issues, he claims it might be a holdover from his rigorous Catholic upbringing. "Growing up I was told that sex is sinful. Imagine what the nuns would say if they saw me last Saturday night in that Pioneer Square dungeon. Guilt and shame are the most powerful restraints ever!"

As upsetting as his unresolved issues from his Catholic past are, they pale in comparison to how deceitful he feels keeping his family in the dark about his kinky life. He is very close to both his mother and sister. They regularly pester him for reasons why he is leaving this string of unhappy women in his wake. "I tell them it is simply a matter of chemistry, which is the truth, just not the whole truth. I rue the day when my family corners me with irrefutable proof of my pervy life. It's only a matter of time till this happens."

Using this Workbook

If you are reading this, you already know that our society can be awfully hostile toward unconventional sexual expressions. And unless you live in a large cosmopolitan city, few opportunities exist for kinksters and other sexual minorities to connect with others in a purposeful way.

Well, all that is about to change. This workbook offers an interactive method for providing practical information and the tools you'll need to maintain and deepen your kinky, BDSM, and alt relationships.

You will learn to address your concerns within a framework of honesty, activity, alliance, support, and humor. And most importantly, you'll be learning how to navigate through this territory *with* and *from* some of the best possible teachers available—other people just like you.

One of the most innovative aspects of this workbook is its format. As a reader, you will be included in an on-the-page workshop, which simulates participation in an actual four-week workshop conducted by Richard Wagner, Ph.D., clinical sexologist and relationship counselor for over 30 years.

You will be offered practical information on the nuts and bolts of successfully living healthy and life-affirming kinky, BDSM, and alt relationships. And we believe this will considerably improve your chances of having long-term success. As in one of Richard's real-life workshops, you will be exposed to authentic life situations that arise when people consciously face their kinkiness in our sex-negative society. You will gain insight and perspective into myriad issues relating to developing effective communication skills. In addition, a panel of skilled practitioners will present important and timely information that is full of humor, encouragement, and compassion. All is designed to help you develop your alt relationships while making the process less intimidating and more enriching.

You'll find everything you need to become an active participant in this process right here in this workbook.

My Check-In

Each of the following chapters represents one of the weeks of this four-week workshop, and each week begins with an opportunity to check-in. This provides each fictional participant a chance to share with the rest of us. In the "My Check-In" section that follows, you'll be offered that same opportunity. You'll also be able to respond to the issues raised in the previous chapter and talk about how they impact your life.

My Turn

In each chapter we'll tackle a specific issue, such as:

- creating healthy alt relationships
- tools for maintaining those relationships
- developinghealthycommunication skills
- strategies for problem solving

You'll be immersed in the discussion your fellow participants have as they come to grips with their own concerns. In the "My Turn" section that follows, you'll be offered an opportunity to join the discussion. You'll have plenty of opportunity to detail your thoughts and inner dialogue and respond to the other group members and to our presenters.

Exercises and At-Home Work

Each chapter contains creative exercises and inventories to further your involvement in the particular subject being addressed. You'll be able to join in with the other participants as they tackle these thought-provoking exercises right along with you.

At the end of each chapter there is an "At-Home Work" section. You will be presented with an activity that is designed to keep you engaged in the process all week long. It will also prepare you for the following week's topic.

Some Final Thoughts

Here are a few suggestions on how to enhance your involvement in this process. First, walk through the process step-by-step just as it's presented. A great deal of thought has gone into producing this program. It moves from one topic to another in a specific order. For optimum success, we suggest that you allow yourself plenty of time and space not only to read through each chapter, but also to complete each exercise and assignment.

One of the best ways to stay involved in this program is by keeping a personal journal. This will serve as your own personal compass throughout the process and will also help you monitor your progress.

This workbook is only able to provide you with a limited amount of space for your reflections and comments, so you may want to keep your journal handy for jotting down all your thoughts, observations, and questions that may not fit on the page provided. By the time you complete this process, you will have a valuable tool for breaking open numerous discussions with your intimate partner(s) or to share with others.

Even though this book provides you with a ten-person on-the-page group, there is no substitute for live human interaction. In light of this, you may wish to invite friends or partners to join you in this process. If you work with someone else we suggest that you read aloud the check-in and discussion portions of each chapter and then, after completing that week's exercises and assignments, you could share your responses with each other.

This is an ideal way to break open a healthy conversation on what it means to live your kinky, BDSM, and alt relationships wisely and well.

Anybody who believes that the way to a man's heart is through his stomach flunked geography.

Robert Byrne

Week 1

From The Ground Up

Welcome and Introductions

Richard: I am so glad you are here. Thank you for joining us.

Before we get started, I'd like to walk you through a few ground rules. This is a workshop, not a therapy group. We're not here to fix anyone or anything. We're here to learn from one another.

Begin today by taking responsibility for this group. It's your group. The more you invest, the richer and more meaningful the experience will be for all of us.

Whatever we discuss here is confidential.

I suggest that you take some time to prepare yourself for each session. One of the best ways to do so is by keeping a journal. Write about your experiences, jot down thoughts and ideas, make a list of topics you want to ask about or discuss.

Each session will begin with a brief round robin check-in. This is an opportunity for you to share your thoughts and comments with the rest of us.

I encourage you to keep an open mind about what you will encounter during this workshop. Even if you've only been part of the scene for a little while, you will have noticed that each person's kinky life is unique. The wonderful diversity that gives our community its richness can also be very confounding. For example, there is no lexicon or dictionary that we all can turn to for definitive definitions of even the most basic terms, like Master or Mistress, slave, Dom or Domme, sub, switch, primary, Top, bottom, lifestyler or polyamorous. So if one of your fellow participants uses a term that you don't understand, or uses it in a way that is unfamiliar to you, ask for clarification. You may be pleasantly surprised at how enriching this sharing can be.

Finally, I also encourage you to keep a sense of humor about what we do and say here. Despite the fact that we will be dealing with a lot of very important issues, and our stories and concerns will, no doubt, be poignant, it's important to remember that all of this is fundamentally about play.

These next few weeks will be jammed with things to do and things to think about. I suggest that you pace yourself. Honor your limits, but don't be afraid to stretch. I promise you won't break.

This process is tried and true. Dozens of other people, just like you, have already completed what you are about to begin. In fact, those who have completed one of these workshops have helped fine-tune it and are now proud to be part of bringing it to you. So if the going gets tough, try to imagine all the other people who trod this same ground before you. It has been a challenge, in one way or another, for every one of them. After all, what kind of adventure would this be if there were no risks involved?

So relax. You're in good company. And welcome to our workshop. Everyone is eager to meet you!

Checking In

Richard: We will begin each session with a round robin check-in. This week I'll ask you to introduce yourselves. Mention what brings you to the group and what expectations you have of our time together. Would you begin for us, Seiko?

Seiko: Hello, my name is Seiko. I'm an East Coast gal. I moved here from New York not quite two years ago. I come from a very traditional family, so moving this far away from home has freed me up in many respects. This is both scary and refreshing.

I'm very new to the scene. And I can thank my good friend and roommate, Xiang, for showing me the ropes, so to speak. I'm here to learn whatever I can about living a kinky life and being honest in the relationships I develop in the scene.

Oh, I'm 29.

Stan: I'll go next. My name's Stan. I'm 52. I'm divorced, and have been for three years.

I've been interested in BDSM for as long as I can remember. Unfortunately, my wife didn't share my interests. In fact, she thought they were disgusting. So now you know why I'm divorced.

I'm looking to make a connection, develop a relationship actually, with a dominant kinky woman. I think I have lots to offer. I'm settled and successful, and the lady would want for nothing. But I have a feeling I'm too old. I can't make heads or tails out of dating nowadays. To tell you the truth, I wasn't all that suave when I was dating my wife, and that was a million years ago. I feel like a dinosaur.

I'm hoping I'll meet this elusive kinky woman through this workshop. I just want to get on with it.

Gretchen: Hello, my name is Gretchen and I'm 44 years old. I'm married to the big lug sitting next to me. His name is Eddie. I'm sure he'll introduce himself in a bit.

Anyway, we've been married for 17 years and we're both really happy. We have four kids, all grown now. We've always been kinky, but we had to tread lightly when our kids were in the house. Now that they've all flown the coop, so to speak, we're ready to kick it up a notch or six.

I'm the slave in this M/s relationship and I'm looking forward to living our commitment 24/7. I'm here to learn how to deal with some of the emotional baggage that I have. I'm a pretty hang-loose kinda gal, but I do have jealousy issues I need to get a handle on.

When we saw a flier for this workshop at a play party several weeks ago, we decided we'd give it a whirl. I mean, any program that will help us be even kinkier and enhance our relationship at the same time is gonna work for me.

Eddie: I'm the big lug she was referring to. My name is Eddie and I'm 48.

Ok, so you already know that Gretchen and I have been married 17 years. What she didn't tell you is that both of us had been married before. We made all the mistakes we could the first time around so we wouldn't have to make them again when we hooked up.

<Laughter>

You laugh, but it's true.

Now that our nest is empty, I'm outfitting our basement into a dungeon/ play space. I'm pretty handy in the DIY department. Oh, I should mention that our grownup kids are cool with how Gretchen and I are living our lives. I guess we did a good job raising them.

My interest in this group is to learn some ways to broaden our family without screwing up the wonderful thing Gretchen and I already have. You see, I'm hoping to add another submissive woman to our household. However, I realize this is much easier said than done. There are so many questions, not least of which is, am I leading my marriage into poly?

Willie: I'll go next. My name is Willie and I'm 36. This is my partner... I mean husband, Mark. We're newlyweds! Thank you, Washington State. But we've actually been together over eight years.

I'd guess you could say that we're an unlikely couple. Mark is a blue blood, with a family pedigree. I'm just a blood from the hood, with hardly any family, let alone a pedigree.

Mark and I aren't hardcore, but we're not novices either. We're here... no, I mean I'm here to develop some communication skills. Mark and I get along pretty well most of the time, but when we get into it, look out. Sometimes it seems like we don't even speak the same language. That's all for me right now.

Mark: I'm Mark, the husband. No wait, Willie is the husband. No wait, we're both husbands.

<Laughter>

Is he shooting daggers at me yet?

I told Willie I'd be on my best behavior while we were here. I'm tryin', hun, but even you have to admit the husband thing is kinda nutty.

Wait, I think I just hit on the reason I'm here. Willie and I are both primarily dominant tops, and while we're both versatile, or switch, as they call it now, neither of us is prone to bottom or sub for the other. I think it's some twisted masculinity thing neither one of us has resolved, but I can't say that for sure.

At any rate, I say ditto to what Willie said about communication skills. We're pretty lacking in that department. Ya see I'm like real vocal, and Willie, well he's just so quiet all the time. Sometimes I interpret this as disinterest on his part, even though I know it's not. But then I go and rag on him anyway. It's like sometimes I just wanna mess with him. I'll be the first to admit, it's pretty fucked up. Okay, I'm done.

Sofie: Hi, I'm Sofie. I'm your basic Jewish poly chick. I have two partners. One's a woman and one's a guy. I guess you could say I'm an equal opportunity fuck.

For the most part, my relationships are great—that is, until one of my partners gets territorial. You simply can't do poly if there's not a bank of trust and good will, right?

Since we're being all confessional and shit, I don't have the best track record for establishing ground rules in either of my relationships. And I think that's primarily the reason I signed up for this workshop. I hope I can pick up a strategy or two for being open and honest about my feelings, needs, and desires without bludgeoning my partners with them.

Oh, and I have this wickedly twisted kinky streak that I want to explore. Ideally, I'd love to try a D/s relationship with my partner Caleb. I think he'd make a killer submissive, and not just in the bedroom. But if we're having problems with trust issues in our poly relationship, then is a D/s relationship even possible?

Oh yeah, I'm 31.

Brodie: Hi, I'm Brodie, I'm 28 and I'm from Glasgow. Can you tell?

People ask me all the time, "Are you visiting from Scotland?" They all look at me funny when I tell them, "No, I've lived here, in the US, since I was 15." I guess I still have my brogue. I don't know, is my accent supposed to have disappeared by now, or what?

Anyhow, I'm really looking forward to this workshop. I've been in the scene for two and a half years now, but I think I came out of the womb kinky. I remember stripping and tying up my action figures when I was just a tyke. I used to love seeing the look on my ma's face when she'd discover my handiwork.

The main reason I'm here is, I apparently have some trouble communicating with people... women mostly, about who I really am. And because of this breakdown in communication, I almost always wind up breaking some poor girl's heart. I think I'm being straightforward about my sexual interests, but maybe I'm not.

Oh, and I'm like totally in the closet about my kinky life with the two most important people in my life, my ma and my sis. This doesn't sit well with me, but I do it anyway. I hope to get some help with this stuff during our time together. That's it for me.

Alicia: Hello, my name's Alicia. I'm 26 years old. I'm like a total newbie to the scene.

My friend and play partner Blake, here, and I met at a play party about a year ago. And like you, Seiko, I'm just beginning to feel my way through this amazingly diverse community.

A couple of years ago, I knew nothing about being kinky. In fact, the only reason I went to that play party, where I met Blake, was because someone dared me to. I thought, *Ok, how weird could it be?*

So now that I'm sorta getting the hang of things, thanks to a bunch of hands-on classes and demos we've been doing together, I'm now able to say, with some confidence, what I like and don't like. Most of the time I bottom or am the sub in play. But I have a feeling that will change with time. As my dungeon skills improve, I'm beginning to sense that I have this inner Domme just waiting to bust out and take charge.

So you probably want to know why I'm here? Well, Blake and I aren't a couple, at least not in the traditional sense of that word. But we are deeply connected through our fascination with BDSM. I don't want to talk for Blake, but I think we need to figure out where we go from here. We also have some relationship issues to address if we're going to continue down this road together. Or maybe we just need to be honest with one another about what kind of relationship we want to have with each other. It's like we both get all balled up with trying to make old, vanilla relationship rules apply to our newfound lives as kinksters. Ya know what I mean?

Blake: Hi, my name is Blake and I'm here because... well, what Alicia said. I don't think I can say it any better than how she said it, so I won't even try.

The way I see it is I'm involving myself in all this really great new BDSM and alt stuff. Hardly a week goes by when Alicia and I aren't off to another class or demo. We're learning so much about the nuts and bolts of power exchange and BDSM. I know how to tie Shibari knots, wield a flogger, and I've even experimented with needle play. But, until we found this workshop, we hadn't seen anything about how to build long-lasting kinky relationships. I mean, what's the use of learning all these great play skills if you don't know how to connect with people and build healthy relationships?

By the way, I just turned 33 a week ago.

Richard: Thank you everyone for your honesty. What a wonderfully diverse group.

I guess this is as good a place as any for me to introduce myself.

My name is Richard Wagner. I'm a sex therapist and a relationship counselor and I've been in private practice since 1981. I'm also an author, sex-positive advocate, and syndicated online sex advice columnist. Here's a little known fact: I'm the only Catholic priest in the world with a doctorate in human sexuality. I know, kinky, huh?

The Catholic Church and I parted ways many, many moons ago. We just couldn't make our relationship work. They demanded my total submission, but I couldn't, or better, wouldn't acquiesce. It was a consent thing. All this ecclesiastical wrangling began when I completed my post-graduate work with the publication of my doctoral thesis concerning the sexual attitudes and behaviors of gay Catholic priests in the active ministry, in 1981. It was unprecedented research back then (and even now, for that matter). There was a firestorm of international publicity. I became known as "The Gay Priest." As if I was the only one. Yeah, right! Needless to say, this notoriety (some say infamy) effectively ended my public ministry. I fought the Vatican for the next thirteen years in an attempt to salvage my priesthood, but the writing was on the wall. I was dismissed from my religious community in 1994, after being a member for twenty-five years.

While I no longer practice as a priest, my thorny experience with the Church, as well as all my years in private practice, has sensitized me to the difficulties sexual minorities, like myself, face in the dominant culture. I've made it my life's work to better this situation for us all. This is what led me to provide workshops like this one.

I firmly believe that social change begins with individuals, and while I am happy to be your guide throughout the coming weeks, the lion's share of the work will fall to you. This process works because each of you will be one another's mentor. I firmly believe that you are the best resource for those who join you here. You see, I am of the mind that the cumulative wisdom of our community, even amongst those who are just starting out, is enormous. And all we have to do is tap into that.

My Check-In

Richard: Take all the time and space you need to introduce yourself to the group. What brings you here? What are your expectations? Would you like to respond to any of your fellow participants?

Workshop

Richard: Ok, let's get to work.

As you know, this workshop is for individuals, couples, and families who identify as kinky. We are here to learn some skills and develop some tools for strengthening our alt relationships by integrating our eroticism and sex play into our daily lives. This workshop is also intended for anyone who wants to start a new relationship, or take an existing relationship to the next level. And most important, it is open to anyone regardless of gender identity, sexuality, or kink interests.

Over the next four weeks we will be addressing a number of important issues. Among them:

- How to find like-minded partners and how to establish healthy, life-affirming relationship habits with these partners
- How to identify and put in place the skills necessary for long-term relationship success
- How to maintain and deepen our alt relationships using BDSM, sex, and kink
- How to effectively ask for what we want and get what we ask for
- How to develop problem solving skills, especially as they apply to kinky, BDSM, and alt relationships

Our time together will conclude on Week 4 with a panel of skilled practitioners representing a variety of relationship structures and kinky interests who will share their perspectives with us. We will have plenty of opportunity to ask questions and to pick their brains. As I said, the cumulative wisdom of our community is enormous. We just need to tap into it.

Let's begin by asking ourselves what *is* the nature of attraction, sex, love, and long-term relationships. Let's see if we can answer the question: *Why do we seek relationships in the first place?*

Blake: Well, as primates, humans are basically social creatures. And everything in the popular culture supports the notion that a solitary life is “wrong” or inherently less fulfilling.

Sofie: I suppose that’s true, but from my point of view, what the dominant culture is selling is a fabrication. We are told that the only alternative to a life lived alone is the monogamous heterosexual model. I reject the idea that this is the only, or even the best, relationship model for many people, myself included. As messed up as my poly life is, from time to time, I wouldn’t change it for the world.

Gretchen: I think that the kind of relationships we seek most often depends on what motivates us to seek them out in the first place, right?

I mean, if I’m simply looking for comfort, affirmation, or companionship, I might be able to find that stuff with someone or some group of people I’m not particularly intimate with. My parents, for example, were totally into the Church. They both found comfort, affirmation, and companionship there, but of course, there was no sex involved.

So I guess what I’m saying is, some people don’t need an exclusive, intimate, sexual connection with someone in order to get a lot of this stuff.

Eddie: Yeah, but when ya add sexual intimacy to the equation, the search is fundamentally altered.

I think Blake’s right. Like our primate relatives, we have the capacity to set up all kinds of different social interactions—friendships, couples, families, and troops, etc. And throughout human history, we’ve developed many intimate relationship models—monogamous, polygamous, and polyamorous, to mention a few. Of course, here in the West we are indoctrinated from childhood that sexual companionship is, like Sofie suggested, only supposed to happen with one person at a time and within a committed relationship. We call that marriage.

Willie: And not only that, but our relationship partners have to be with people of the correct gender. Same-sex coupling, even if it’s an exclusive, monogamous connection, is still prohibited most places.

Stan: And don't forget all the negative repercussions when that marriage fails. Someone is always at fault.

I caught so much shit from my ex-wife's friends when we broke up. Of course, she had to tell all our friends that I was this sicko because I was kinky. It beats the shit out of me.

Brodie: I hear ya on that, Stan. And ya know what? You don't even have to be married to someone for the shit to hit the fan when things go belly-up.

I've blown through more than a few relationships with girlfriends in the past couple of years. The end of each of these relationships has been extremely unpleasant.

And you're right about the stuff people say about you when the relationship is over. My ex-girlfriends have all talked trash about me and my kinky interests. It's massive.

Richard: Good work you guys! I'm delighted that we started this discussion by looking at the relationship models we see in the natural world. There's some wisdom in that. In short order we've uncovered several different reasons why we, as primates, seek out relationships and the many forms these interactions take.

Alicia: I remember my first love. I was just a teenager. We were together for just a few months before it blew up in our faces. I was so devastated. I remember reading somewhere how the end of a relationship can be like a death in the family. We pass through the five stages of grief: Denial, Anger, Bargaining, Depression, and finally Acceptance. That was comforting at the time. I thought to myself, *Maybe I'll get through this.* And so I did.

Richard: True enough! But it's equally interesting to note how resilient we humans can be. Despite the pain associated with the end of a relationship, most of us get right back up on that horse and resume dating.

I suggest there is a reason for this resilience. Maybe it's the positive reinforcements we get from relationships that keep us coming back for more. But there are also a slew of "feel-good" chemicals that flood our brain when we fall in love. These chemicals give us that feeling of bliss, that sense of elation and wellbeing. Our hearts race, our skin flushes, our palms sweat. Researchers say this is due to the dopamine, norepinephrine and phenylethylamine our brain is releasing. Curiously enough, BDSM aficionados speak in similar terms about the role of endorphins and adrenaline in power exchange.

This suggests to me that, for the most part, the positive reinforcement, both social and physiological, trumps the negatives when things go wrong or fail entirely. And so we pick ourselves up, dust ourselves off, and look for that "high" somewhere else.

Mark: You're right! That sounds remarkably like what they call "sub-space."

Richard: Exactly so!

Consider for a moment the evolutionary nature of lust and love. Lust evolved to promote mating, while love evolved to promote bonding—partner for partner and infant for mother, etc. So even though we often experience lust for our romantic partners, sometimes we don't. And that's okay. Or maybe we lust after more than one person at a time. I think that's normal too.

Sofie: Maybe that's why polyamorous relationships are so fulfilling for some of us. We're able to experience the full range of feelings possible from intimate relationships. And when I say intimacy, I'm not necessarily talking about sex.

Richard: It's clear from what we know about sexual attraction that lustful passion often interferes with our ability to think rationally—at least when it comes to the objects of our attraction. The old saying "love is blind" is really accurate at this stage of attraction. We are often oblivious to the flaws our partners might have. We idealize them and can't get them off our minds. This overwhelming preoccupation is part of our biology. Some researchers call this limerence or love sickness.

Brodie: Well this explains a lot. I guess when a chick is all in love, she may overlook the other messages that come to her about her potential lover. Like when I tell her I'm kinky. These words either don't connect with her, or she thinks the power of romantic love will overcome this inconvenient obstacle.

Willie: It's not only a chick thing, I can assure you of that.

Richard: You're both spot on!

During this romantic passion phase, couples spend hours and hours getting to know each other. If this attraction remains strong and mutually felt, then they usually enter the third stage, which is attachment.

The attachment, or commitment, stage is what holds the relationship together. Once passed the fantasy love stage, we open ourselves to something more substantial. This stage of love has to be strong enough to withstand the many problems and distractions we are faced with on a daily basis.

Studies show that the more we idealize the one we love, the stronger the pair bond, at least during the attachment stage.

Seiko: I see where you are going with this, but doesn't this also have a darker side? When the romantic passion "blinders" come off, as they inevitably do, doesn't the love object dissolve in the eyes of the infatuated one?

Mark: I was wondering the same thing.

Richard: Yes, I think that is true. I guess it just goes to show that nothing is for certain.

Let's push deeper into this, shall we?

As you all probably know, there is a power dynamic in every human relationship. We, like all animals, naturally work out the "pecking order" with every other human we meet. Sometimes this is effortless. We simply go with the flow. The conventions of modern living do a lot of the work for us. Stopping at a red light, for example, is an act of submission to the drivers who have a green light. However, sometimes the arrangement isn't as obvious, or people outgrow a power structure. When that happens a struggle ensues; for example, a teenager rebelling against her parents.

Since we are also social animals living in groups, this hierarchical structure is often very obvious. We have authority figures in every walk of life—

bosses, religious superiors, parents, teachers, older siblings, and the list goes on and on. A person can be dominant in one situation and submissive in the next. Dominance and submission are integral parts of life. In fact, they are so integrated into everything we do that we rarely question them.

Now, those of us who harness this natural power dynamic in our alt culture and play add yet another layer to our interactions with others. Our conscious use of this dynamic is by consent; we agree to dominate and/or submit.

And with this in mind, I'd like to press on with our first exercise.

Exercise 1 — A Personal Alt-Relationship Inventory

I'd like each of you to create a list of the following:

- What are my specific alt-relationship goals?

- How do I evaluate my success in reaching these goals?

- What are the advantages of an alt relationship?

- What are the responsibilities of an alt relationship?

- What problems arise in your alt relationship(s)?

- How do you deal with these problems?

Take as much time as you need to complete this exercise. We'll pick up our discussion when you've finished.

Richard: All finished? Good.

Let's see what you've come up with. How did you respond to the first question: **What are my specific alt-relationship goals?**

Who wants to begin?

Gretchen: I'll start. This was real easy for me. I want to live my M/s relationship with Eddie 24/7. I want to celebrate my collaring with friends and family. I am proud to be his slave. This power exchange relationship, with its protocols and rules, says love and romance to me. It's not a traditional expression of these feelings, by any means, but it works for me.

Mark: Unlike Gretchen, I was stumped by this question. Actually all these questions perplexed me. I guess that's why I'm here, to try and figure these things out.

Willie: Same here. I mean it's pretty easy for Mark and me to decide who's in charge when we're doing normal stuff, like I'm the boss in the kitchen. Mark is the decorator. We both acknowledge and respect on another's roles. It's when we try to duke it out for sexual supremacy that our problems arise.

I mean, is it even possible for two dominant males to live in harmony?

Richard: Well, you guys have a successful eight-year relationship under your belt, so whatever you are doing must be working on some level, right? I encourage you not to critique what you have together using someone else's criteria. This is all about you finding your own way and establishing your own relationship model.

But to answer your question, yes, two dominant personalities can live together in harmony. However, for that to happen the individuals involved must know how to communicate effectively. And there must be an underlying commitment to flexibility and patience.

Let's move on to the second question—**How do I evaluate my success in reaching these goals?**

Stan: I suck at achieving my relationship goals. I'm so depressed.

I don't know, the harder I try to realize my dream of hooking up with a dominant, kinky woman, the less successful I am.

Richard: Ya know what, Stan? I think you've got this whole D/s thing backwards. A dominant woman finds her submissive, not the other way around.

If you want to attract the attention of a Domme, well then, make yourself as appealing as possible. You said something in your introduction that may hold the key. You said you have lots to offer: "I'm settled and successful and the lady would want for nothing." That, my friend, may very well be your ticket out of the doldrums. However, your attitude is as important as the things you bring to the table. If you're a braggart or if you try to "buy" the attentions of the woman you want to connect with, you will shoot yourself in the foot. But if your attitude is humble and respectful you might have a real shot at this.

Begin by asking yourself: *What concrete things can I offer a prospective partner that would make me stand out as the ideal submissive for this particular woman?*

Seiko: I think Richard's right, Stan. Maybe all you need to do is hone your submissive skills. I mean, if we met at a party, I'm pretty sure I'd be interested in you. However, I'd lose interest mighty fast once I got wind of your defeatist attitude.

Like Mark and Willie, I'm still trying to figure out what this all means in my life. I know, for example, that I defer to Xiang in just about everything to do with the culture. She simply has more experience than me. But my interaction with her is also colored by the strong affectionate feelings I have for her. Does this make me a sub?

Richard: I think there's more to being a sub than simply being in love with someone and deferring to that person. Being a sub or a slave is a conscious choice and a self-identification. Behaving in one fashion or another doesn't make one dominant or submissive, at least not in alt-culture terms.

This gets us to the next question: **What are the advantages of an alt relationship?**

Eddie: I put down the word "clarity." For me clarity is the most important advantage of my M/s relationship with Gretchen. I feel comfortable knowing what my role as the Master and head of our household entails. Oddly enough, I never had that clarity when my job description was simply "husband."

Our structured relationship also stimulates the sexual connection I have with Gretchen. She is my consensual sex slave; it's just one of the services she provides me.

Blake: I agree with Eddie. Knowing what is expected of me at any given time is, for lack of a better term, liberating. In fact, I'm beginning to reevaluate my self-identification as a top. It's pretty clear to me that I'm not all that dominant most of the time. And it's too exhausting trying to be something I'm not when nobody is pressuring me to be one thing or another.

Sometimes when I bottom during play, I feel incredibly submissive. I'm beginning to think that this is way more than just a submissive streak. And I'm not sure I know what to do with this newfound information.

I also see the potential for more intense communication, transparency, and honesty as an advantage of an alt relationship.

Alicia: I'm so happy to hear you say that, Blake. I've been sensing your dissatisfaction, but I didn't know what to say about that. Maybe I need to be more supportive of this discernment process you are going through. But damn, I just don't know how.

I'm not sure I know what to call this, but I put down that I don't have to second-guess someone's self-identification as the greatest advantage of an alt relationship. Our self-designations are like having a kind of shorthand, aren't they? Depending on our self-identification, we can skip a lot of the all-too-coy "getting-to-know-ya" bullshit and get down to business.

Of course, as I'm just discovering, this shorthand sometimes means people get trapped in a role that no longer fits them.

Richard: Exactly! Here's a thought. You and Blake may want to try a simple role-reversal exercise. Choose a specific day where the two of you agree that one or the other of you will be dominant while the other will be submissive. Then on another occasion, switch roles. This exercise will allow each of you to explore the D/s dynamic from both sides, as it were. Does that make sense?

Remember, none of this stuff has to be carved in stone.

Ok, who wants to weigh in with the next question: **What are the responsibilities of an alt relationship?**

Brodie: For me the responsibilities are all centered on my being the best Master I can be. I'm committed to becoming as skillful a Dom as humanly possible. This means perfecting my leadership skills, dungeon skills, and sexual skills. I don't want to simply don a leather vest and say, "Look at me, I'm a Master." There's altogether too much of that already going on in the scene.

And to be honest, I totally get off on the rituals and protocols. There is such a rich and diverse history to our community and I love hearing the lore. It's like belonging to a secret society.

Sofie: The main responsibility, as I see it, is being honest and vocal about my needs, desires, and expectations. I still struggle with this, but it is my goal.

One of the things I've noticed in my limited time in the scene is that people in the culture tend to be more open to different relationships structures—monogamy, polyamory, play partners, leather families, and tribes, etc. I love it!

My male partner Caleb and I have yet to actually try a D/s relationship, but I sense the interest is there. I never feel inhibited about exploring my kinks, or his. Maybe that's because our relationship is mostly a sex connection. I think it comes with the territory.

Alicia: For me, as a sub, the responsibilities center around service, obedience, and sexual skills. I know that this word keeps coming up, but I'll use it anyway. Communication is key.

The thing is, most of us haven't any training on how to communicate effectively in our day-to-day lives, let alone in our culture lives. It seems to me that when a difficulty arises we... I mean I, revert to old habits of blaming and shaming. It's very disappointing when it happens, but it happens nonetheless.

Richard: Let's see what you guys have for this question: **What problems arise in your alt relationship(s)?**

Willie: I put down one word: negotiation. I don't know how to negotiate for what I want, need, and desire, nor do I know how to negotiate for Mark's wants, needs, and desires. I swear, it's the biggest bugaboo in my relationship.

Sometimes it seems as though I'm just being contrary. Mark wants something, I withhold. It's like a game I play.

Mark: I'm equally to blame for this.

It's not like I don't know how to negotiate; I do. My professional life is completely dependent on my negotiating skills, and I'm really good at it, but I don't carry that skill into my marriage or any of my other alt relationships.

I get my hackles up when I don't get my own way. My mother is right; I am a spoiled brat. I know this is destructive and I know it hurts Willie, but I do it anyway. It's selfishness, pure and simple.

Stan: Ok, this is beginning to creep me out. It's weird hearing you talk about your "marriage," as if it's a real marriage, like between a man and a woman. Just sayin'.

Richard: Your personal prejudices are getting in the way of you participating in this exercise, Stan. Why don't you focus on the task at hand?

You said at the outset that you're not having any success achieving your relationship goals. You say you are depressed about this. Let's try and uncover what's going wrong for you and why you can't connect with the kinky women you seek.

Stan: Sorry if I offended anyone. My wife used to accuse me of being a real boor. Maybe she was right.

Anyhow, I suppose you could say my little outburst exemplifies how my social skills work. I don't mean to be rude, but that's how I come across a lot of the time.

For example, last month I met this dominant woman online and chatted her up. We were meeting online for a couple of weeks and I really thought we were onto something. She was smart, funny, a kick-ass top with lots of experience and she seemed to like me. We exchanged photos, nothing explicit mind you, just our faces. Then we decided to meet for coffee.

I arrived at the café first. A little while later she walked in. Her face looked just like she looked in the photo she sent me, which was great. But the rest of her, holy cow! She was fat! Not obscenely obese, more like plump. And that's the first thing I said to her. I said, "I didn't know you were fat." That was the end of that. She didn't even sit down. She called me a asshole and left.

Brodie: Dude, that was so not cool!

Sofie: Seriously? You called a woman you were meeting for the first time fat? Had you done that to me, I would've kicked you in the balls. What were you thinking? What a douche!

Stan: I didn't mean to hurt her feelings. I was just being honest.

Eddie: But you did hurt her feelings! And no one has the right to be blatantly honest in a hurtful way like that.

Here's a tip, Stan. The kinky community is big and diverse, but it is also small and insulated. If word gets out that you're a social fuck-up you will never meet dominant women in this town ever again.

Let me ask, when you say you didn't mean to hurt her feelings, are you saying a) You didn't think before you spoke? Or b) You didn't know that calling a woman fat to her face at your first meeting is a no-no?

The reason I ask is, if the answer is "a," then you need to learn how to better monitor yourself. But if the answer is "b," then you need to crawl back under the rock from whence you came.

Now that's me being honest with you!

Richard: Let's try to keep this conversation as constructive as possible, shall we? Stan, do you get what your friends here are trying to tell you? What are your reactions?

Stan: I know, it's fucked. By the time I realized what had happened and tried to apologize, she was gone.

I just get nervous. The anticipation of meeting a Dominatrix makes me a little crazy.

I'm beginning to think that my expectations are too high. I watch a lot of BDSM porn, and all the dominant women in the movies are slim and beautiful. I want one like that.

Gretchen: Well, there's your problem right there. The movies aren't real. And are you really that shallow? Is porn star beauty your only criterion for a happy connection with a dominant woman?

I have a little suggestion. Maybe at some point during this workshop you and I could do a little role-playing. I think I might be able to help you with some of these issues.

Richard: That's a great idea. Thank you, Gretchen.

Finally, there's the question: **How do you deal with these problems?**

Sofie: This is probably not what you want to hear, but my default way of handling a difficult situation is to pick a fight. I know it sounds crazy, but that's what I do.

Since I don't really know how to set boundaries and my communication skills are negligible, fighting seems like the only other alternative. The upside to this dysfunctional approach is there is often really great make-up sex afterward.

<Laughter>

Mark: Now that you mention it, that's my modus operandi too. I think subconsciously I'm hoping that a good verbal brawl will distract Willie's attention from my inability to be honest with him. Dumb, huh?

Eddie: You guys knock me out. I totally recognize that behavior, because I used to do it all the time in my first marriage. Of course, I was only 21 at the time.

Happily, nowadays Gretchen and I take a more civilized approach to problem solving. We went to a class a number of years ago and learned to actively listen to one another. This technique was taught as part of a Fair Fighting workshop. It's done wonders for our marriage and our M/s relationship too.

Seiko: I'm more of an avoider. That's how everyone in my family deals with problems. I come from a long line of very skilled Japanese avoiders.

Avoiding unpleasantness never resolves the problem; it just puts it into deep freeze.

My roommate Xiang is the total opposite of me. She is constantly in my face about every little thing. I am so not used to this and I find it incredibly intimidating. I often want to run and hide.

There's got to be a happy medium between total avoidance and total confrontation, right?

Brodie: I don't know if this is what you are asking with that question, Richard, but after numerous relationship disasters with girlfriends, I've started telling my dates upfront that I'm kinky. It's now a part of my first-date discussion. The funny thing is, I, more often than not, get something like, "Kinky? How can that be, you're so preppy looking."

As soon as I hear that, I know I'm in trouble.

Sofie: I used to have that same problem, Brodie. The vanilla people I used to date couldn't believe a nice Jewish girl like me was polyamorous and bisexual. It used to freak them out. Or I became this challenge. "I can cure you of that," they'd say. As if!

Now I only date inside the poly and bi community. It doesn't eliminate the problem all together, but the issues are more manageable.

Richard: So to sum up, if we want the candy (the advantages of our alt relationships) we need to earn it. All relationships involve work, and kink relationships involve even more work.

We have a responsibility to learn how to overcome outmoded or destructive habits of interacting with one another. Like Sofie said a little while ago, blaming, shaming, dishonesty, and failing to own or take responsibility for our shortcomings is what kills the possibility for long-term relationship success.

My Turn

Richard: What did this exercise uncover for you about your relationship goals? What are your successes? Where do you need more help?

Richard: Sorry about interrupting this great discussion, but our time for today is just about up. And there's some homework I want to distribute. This week's exercise will help you keep this inner dialogue going until we meet again.

If you want to incorporate a partner or family member in this process, feel free to do so. Or if you want to keep this to yourself for now, that's cool too. Either way, put some time and energy into it, and when we return next week we'll review our responses to the exercise.

Thanks so much for your lively participation. It's been great getting to know each of you a bit better.

AT-HOME WORK

Week 1 — Personality Characteristics Exercise

First, choose five words, from the following list, that you believe best describe you. Then prioritize them in the order of importance. Your first word should be the word you most identify with.

Second, explain why you picked the words you did and why you prioritized them in the order you did.

Feel free to add words to the master list if you think other words better describe you than those on this list.

Humble	Risk-Taker	Charming
Patient	Analytical	Daring
Admirable	Confrontational	Methodical
Persuasive	Approachable	Indirect
Generous	Insensitive	Resistant to change
Bold	Team player	Indecisive
Diplomatic	Individualistic	Thorough
Kind	Direct	Conscientious
Forceful	Inspiring	Perfectionist

Impulsive	Enthusiastic	Avoid details
Predictable	Pessimistic	Good communicator
Accurate	Optimistic	Demanding
Competitive	Disorganized	Good time manager
Sociable	Organized	Poor time manager
Deliberate	Good listener	Honest
Agreeable	Poor listener	Cooperative
Decisive	Empathetic	Avoid deadlines
Logical	Systematic	Dependable
Tactful	Focused	Avoid ambiguity
Contented	Well-disciplined	Respectful
Precise	Fearful	Controlled
Detail-oriented	Gentle	Careful
Articulate	Critical thinker	Courteous
Challenging	Popular	People-oriented
Task-oriented	Joyful	Charming

Entertaining	Friendly	Talkative
Fun-loving	Cheerful	Outspoken
Persuasive	Extroverted	Introverted
Persistent	Adventurous	Humorous
Pioneering	Stubborn	Aggressive
Timid	Bold	Argumentative
Insistent	Problem solver	Strong-willed
Forceful	Determined	Confident
Independent	Daring	Self-assured
Practical	Helpful	Energetic
Trustworthy	Loyal	Easygoing
Conservative	Liberal	Objective
Subjective		

"Life in Lubbock, Texas, taught me two things: One is that God loves you and you're going to burn in hell. The other is that sex is the most awful, filthy thing on earth and you should save it for someone you love."

Butch Hancock

Week 2

Making It Work

Checking In

Richard: Welcome back, everyone. Let's begin today with our check in. This week I'll ask you to focus your attention on last week's homework exercise and what it brought up for you. Who would like to begin?

Blake: I'd like to begin if I that's all right.

First, I'd like to say that I really liked the *Personality Characteristics Exercise*, but it was also very challenging.

To begin with, I picked through the master list of words and collected as many of them that I thought fit me. When I finished, I discovered, to my dismay, that I had collected more than a dozen words to describe myself. It was a bitch to narrow that list down to just five. And it was even harder to pick out just one word. Can someone really sum up the totality of who he is in just one word?

Ok, so maybe the task wasn't meant to sum up myself in a single word, but that's what it felt like. I'd like to know if anyone else had the same difficulties I did.

Anyway, my final five-word list came down to: **Agreeable, Methodical, Predictable, Trustworthy,** and **Practical**. And I arranged them in descending order of importance as the exercise requested. When I use them all together like this, they capture more of me and I feel better. Like I said, choosing a single word was the hardest part.

I chose **Agreeable**, as the single word that best describes me because that was the most open-ended word on my original list of twelve.

That's it for me.

Brodie: At first I thought this exercise was going to be a snap. Unlike you, Blake, I understood the directions to say that my list of five words should be words I identify with. I'm not sure that's the same thing as describing oneself, but maybe it is.

Anyway, my words are these: **Persuasive, Popular, Well-disciplined, Risk-taker,** and **Bold**.

I really like how they sound together. I like to think I own these words and they are me.

Ranking them in the order of importance was the harder part. I had the damnedest time deciding if I was more persuasive or popular. I finally decided on **Persuasive**, because popular seemed so shallow. Does this just boil down to vanity? I wonder.

After looking at all the words on the list I'm glad I could choose the ones that I did. I hope they convey that I'm a take-charge kinda guy.

Sofie: Your list of words does sound like you're a take-charge kind of guy, Brodie. My list, on the other hand, sounds like the opposite of that.

Since the instructions that accompanied the exercise said that we could add words to the master list if we thought other words better describe ourselves than those on the list provided, I did just that. But I added just one word.

So here's my list: **Sassy, Impulsive, Liberal, Outspoken,** and **Disorganized**. The word I added was sassy. It wasn't on the list, but it fits me to a tee. I suppose that outspoken and sassy are pretty close, but outspoken doesn't have the edge that sassy does. And I like the edgy part, as you can probably guess.

Once I completed the exercise I showed my list to both my partners, Caleb and Emma, on separate occasions. Emma said I should have chosen disorganized as my main word, but then again she's like totally anal retentive; even Martha Stewart would look disorganized to her. But Emma does have a point. I simply can't be bothered with trivialities.

Caleb, on the other hand, looked puzzled when I showed him my list. He said, "Hey, how come you didn't use the word 'sexy'?" Isn't he sweet? Actually, I think he said that because we haven't seen much of each other the last couple of weeks and he was horny as hell when we finally got together. But at least he thought my choice of sassy was accurate. To reward him for his thoughtfulness I let him massage my feet.

Alicia: I must have rearranged my list a dozen times before I settled on the one I will share with you. I kept choosing words that made me sound like a robot. I mean, all of them were applicable, for sure, but I know I'm way more than that. So then I tried collecting words for another list. Each time I made a list, at least one or two of the following would appear on it: **Critical Thinker, Task-oriented, Problem Solver**. After a while I just decided to keep these three as my core words. I then tried to find a couple of other words that would humanize me a little bit. The two other words I finally settled on were **Adventurous** and **Inspiring**. So, taken together, I like what I see. Sure, my strong suit is being analytical and solving problems, but I also have this other side.

This exercise got me thinking about what we discussed last week. I remember how I fumbled around trying to explain my relationship with Blake and the role I generally take in the culture. As I recall, I said something to the effect that I don't mind bottoming in a scene. But outside of play, I think I'm better suited as the one in charge.

My list of words, **Problem Solver, Critical Thinker, Task-oriented, Adventurous,** and **Inspiring,** really nails it.

No wonder I don't easily fit into one particular pigeonhole. Judging from this exercise, I'd say I have lots of room to expand. That makes me happy.

Seiko: I'm a big fan of word games. Even as a kid, I would entertain myself for hours on end with a word jumble. I can't help it; I'm a geek like that.

Initially, I approached last week's homework like a word puzzle. It wasn't until I showed my finished list to my roommate, Xiang, that it finally dawned on me.

She said, "What is this all about?" I told her that I was doing this workshop and this was a homework exercise. And that's when it hit me. The exercise was supposed to help me figure out my personality type and how that might impact my identification in the culture, right?

Once I figured this out, I went back and tried the exercise again. Curiously enough, I came up with virtually the same list as I did the first time around. I'm not sure I know what that means, but I'm glad that I know myself as well as I do.

So anyhow, this is my list: **Intelligent, Humble, Perfectionist, Conscientious,** and **Tactful.**

I don't really get a strong Dom or sub vibe from my list of words, do you? Gee, I hope I did the exercise right.

Stan: After last week's session I was feeling pretty down about myself. Things began to turn around when Gretchen and I met for coffee mid week. I'll have more to say about this later, but for now I want to share my list of adjectives with you. My words are: **Trustworthy, Generous, Deliberate, Argumentative,** and **Indecisive**.

I like the first three words the most. The last two words take some of the shine off the first three, but I'm pretty ok with that.

Gretchen said I should think of myself as a work in progress, and I know she's right. She also helped me see that the way to get what I want, a relationship with a dominant kinky woman, is through developing my three strongest attributes and learning to control the other two. I think I can do that. Thank you, Gretchen; because of you I am feeling a lot more confident.

Gretchen: After those very nice words, thank you Stan, I guess I'll go next.

I really liked this exercise and it was helpful too. I was surprised to discover how the words I chose to describe myself seemed to jump off the page at me. But there was one missing, and since I wanted this to be as accurate a representation of me as possible, I added a word. Here's my list: **Patient, Enthusiastic, Optimistic, Gentle,** and **Jealous**.

Jealous wasn't on the list, but since I know that this rather unfortunate trait has been with me since I was a kid, it would have been dishonest to leave it off my list. I did, however, take the liberty of putting it at the end of my list because I honestly do try to keep it in check.

I also know that I'm most authentically myself when I'm patient, enthusiastic, optimistic, and gentle. And my life with Eddie, both as his wife and his slave, is relatively effortless when I'm genuinely being me.

In fact, that's exactly what Stan and I talked about at coffee. Syncing up what you want in life with what you are emotionally capable of and then developing a skill set to showcase that capacity is what will get you what you want and make you happy. At least, that's what I think.

So that's it for me.

Eddie: Isn't she amazing? I love this woman. Gretchen is about the wisest person I know. I don't believe there's anything we can't overcome when we pull together.

Speaking of which, I was so surprised when Gretchen and I compared our list of five words. We clearly compliment one another.

This is my list: **Resourceful, Organized, Detail-oriented, Helpful,** and **People-oriented.** I should mention that I added the first word, resourceful, because it wasn't on the master list. It is also the word that best describes me of the five.

When Gretchen and I compared lists she said that she has always been confident that I had her best interest at heart. She said that this is what makes submitting to me so easy and rewarding. I thought about that for a while and I had to agree. I mean, how can anyone ask someone else to submit if the person doing the asking doesn't instill a sense of confidence in the one he wishes to dominate? I mean, if there's no bond of trust, then the power exchange is nothing more than a power trip, right?

I'm done.

Willie: You took the words right out of my mouth, Eddie. This is what I've been struggling with for ages.

When Mark and I got home after last week's session, I suggested that we tweak the assignment a bit. I suggested that we not only follow the instructions that came with the exercise and come up with five words that each of us identified with, but that we should also compile a similar list of five words that each of us thought best described the other. Once we were finished with our two lists, we'd compare notes.

Mark: Willie thought that if we wanted to breakthrough the logjam we are experiencing in our relationship, we needed to take some risks. I was game, so we gave ourselves a couple of days to do the work and then set up a time for us to make the comparison.

Willie: This was a stretch for us both. We had never really done anything like this before. We tend to avoid confrontation until it's too late and then we explode. I figured that this exercise would either indicate a dying relationship or signal a new beginning. One thing for sure, it would get us off dead center.

When the day of reckoning came, we met at the dining room table, note pads in hand. Since I suggested the tweak, I offered to go first by revealing the five words I thought best described me. Here's my list: **Loyal, Approachable, Kind, Honest,** and **Thorough**. I told Mark that I had a tough time with the list, because I don't really like talking about myself.

Mark: It's true! He's the most self-deprecating man I know. I think that's why I sometimes have a hard time hearing him. He's always so reserved and subtle. He is so totally unlike me.

Just take a look at my list: **Daring, Charming, Direct, Confrontational,** and **Poor listener**. Right away you can see how vastly different Willie and I are from one another. And I remind you, this is just how we see ourselves.

Willie: I was totally blown away when I saw that Mark had put poor listener on his list. I saw it on the master list and I put it on my list for him, but I never thought he would own that for himself. I was so proud of him.

Now it was my turn to share the list of five words that I think best describe Mark. I had way more confidence giving him my list, because he had already used the most loaded word on his own list. I handed him my list and asked him to read—**Competitive, Articulate, Fun-loving, Charming,** and **Poor listener**. I told him I wanted to add drop-dead gorgeous, but that wasn't on the master list.

Mark: Besides the poor listener thing, I was so stoked to see that Willie thought so highly of me. I leaned across the table and gave him a big kiss.

I told him, "Ya know, for all of my bravado, deep down inside I'm secretly afraid that no one will like me for who I really am, which includes my flaws."

After we talked about the list he made for me, I handed Willie the list of five words I think best describe him and hoped for the best. It included: **Loyal, Respectful, Focused, Kind,** and **Diplomatic**.

Willie: Mark's list of my qualities knocked me out. Not only did he use two of the very same words I did—kind and loyal—but he also used the same first word as the most accurate word to describe me as I did.

I sat across the table from him and just grinned. I now had proof that Mark has indeed been paying attention. I'm not invisible to him, as I thought I was.

I told him I was ready to redouble my efforts to take our relationship to the next level. If we can just find some tools for keeping this communication momentum going, I know we'll make some serious headway.

Richard: Well done, everyone. I was hoping some of you would have been able to connect this *Personality Characteristics Exercise* with last week's session because that's how I intended it.

I'd like to suggest that we take a short break. Stretch your legs, grab some refreshments, and we'll regroup in fifteen minutes.

My Check-In

Richard: Take all the time and space you need to write about your week. Pay special attention to last week's homework—the *Personality Characteristics Exercise*. What did this bring up for you? Would you like to respond to anyone in the group?

Workshop

Richard: Last week we talked about the nature of attraction, sex, love, and long-term relationships. We looked at the natural power dynamics operative in all human relationships. We took a look at how some of us try to harness this natural power dynamic in our alt relationships and play. We also discovered some of the problems we kinksters face when we add this additional layer to our interactions with others. Despite consciously using this power dynamic by consent—we agree to dominate and/or submit, to top and/or bottom—it's clear that we need more than just consent to make things work.

Like Willie suggested a little while ago, most of us are searching for practical tools to assist us in maintaining and deepening our alt relationships. So this week let's concentrate on that effort, shall we?

I believe we will find the tools we need by first identifying how alt relationships are different from conventional relationships.

Who wants to start us off?

Sofie: There are no pop stars, political figures, or athletes out there waving the freak flag.

Sure, if you hang out in the culture long enough you're bound to meet folks who are making things work, but that's a big if for a lot of us. Most of us have to keep our kinky identities under wraps, and hiding like this creates its own problems.

Vanilla relationships have loads of role models. Most are vapid, but at least they are visible in our society.

Seiko: One thing I've noticed in my short time in the scene is that some people, even those in relationships, sometimes have differing ideas about how their relationships should work. And I suspect that if these differences are left unaddressed, the mismatched expectations will eventually undermine the relationship.

Gretchen: That's what last week's homework brought up for me too. Those of us who identify as kinky or who are in alt relationships need to hammer out all the ground rules for that relationship with everyone who is involved. There is no predetermined formula. And there's got to be an ongoing negotiation process, a process that has to last the lifetime of the relationship.

Like you were saying, Sofie, those in more conventional relationships can fall back on a common set of expectations and legal obligations without having to consciously negotiate them. They simply have to follow societal standards—a husband and wife are expected to support one another financially, for instance. Eddie and I tried to do that in our first marriages, but still it didn't work for us.

But when we got together and formed our M/s relationship, we couldn't look to those societal standards as the starting point in our new relationship. We discovered over the years that we had to create our own way of doing M/s. In the beginning, we learned from others, who walked this path before us. We learned about things like structure, protocols, standing orders, service, and rituals. And thanks to a handful of wonderful friends who shared their strategies with us, we learned how to make this stuff work for us. They were our mentors and role models. Even now Eddie and I will turn to these people for their assistance. For example, we're currently discussing the whole jealousy and polyamory thing with them.

Marching to a different drummer means we are often out of step with those in conventional relationships. It's certainly a whole lot more work, but I think it's worth it. And having a community of like-minded people to turn to for support and encouragement is absolutely essential.

Willie: I know what you mean, Gretchen, you can "go with the flow" for just so long. But at some point, if you expect your relationship to be successful in the long term, you have to take a step back and talk about common goals and expectations. Of course, the key to this is communication. And my question remains: How do we build dynamic and healthy communication habits into our alt relationships?

Richard: Good point, Willie.

So let's take a look at that very question. What does effective communication look like in a healthy alt relationship?

Exercise 1 – Essentials of Effective Communication

What comes to mind for you when you think about effective communication? Jot down a half dozen or so key words or phrases that you think are essential to listening and being heard.

Richard: Ok, are you ready to continue? Good! What's on your list of essentials for healthy communication?

Eddie: I put down: direct, clear verbal messages, and being open and honest.

Alicia: Yeah, those things are important all right. But unless there are good listeners as well as effective communicators all your best intentions will fail. I mean, these things are two sides of the same coin, right?

Mark: Right! That's where I generally dropped the ball.

I told Willie that when he wanted me to really listen to something he had to say, he needed to change his presentation style from his normal quiet, subtle style to something that will get my attention. I really do want to listen to him, but honestly, he has to compete with all the other noise in my head. I have a feeling that if Willie would be more assertive in his presentation style, we could avoid the pitfalls we've been experiencing.

Brodie: I've been trying to learn how to deal with arguments and disagreements in a more rational, calm, and patient way. I know that when I get all riled up in the face of a confrontation, I rapidly lose control of the situation. And I don't want to lose control.

Now I try to breathe through my discomfort and anxiety before I react. And guess where I learned how to do that? Yep, I learned that technique in a bondage class. I mean, think about it, those of us who are into BDSM have learned lots of ways of dealing with uncomfortable and stressful situations. I figure, why leave those lessons in the dungeon when they are equally applicable in my day-to-day life?

Stan: I never thought of that. Makes sense though. I should give that a try.

Like I said earlier, when we were discussing our five words, one word that defines me is argumentative. I've always had a hair-trigger when it comes to an argument, but I know that even if I win an argument, it's often at my own expense. It's like winning the battle but losing the war. That's not good.

Blake: Of course, a lot of communication occurs through body language, gestures, and tone, right?

For example, if my anxiety is showing when I'm talking, if my voice is loud and my pitch is high, I'm probably negating any conciliatory words I may be speaking.

Alicia: I never thought of that, but you're right.

I can think of several other manipulative behaviors too. We've all had to deal with passive-aggressive people, haven't we? These people can only express their emotions indirectly. Things are never what they seem with them.

And I'm sure each of you has heard of that particularly culture-specific no-no—topping from the bottom.

<Laughter>

Richard: Well done!

We have a good list of essentials for healthy communication to work with. Now let's see if we can develop some strategies or tools for making those things part of our everyday life.

I think we can all agree that effective communication is dependent on sending clear, unambiguous messages to our partners and then making sure that our messages are fully understood. But how do we accomplish this?

Willie: I'm trying to use words like I, me, and my when I attempt to express something important. When I do this I feel like I'm taking responsibility for what I'm trying to say. If I use words like "they" or "some people," I disown my own message and shift the responsibility to someone or something else. Of course, this doesn't come naturally to me; it's not my usual way of speaking. So I have to concentrate on the words I use. I just realized that this concentration and thoughtfulness might be what Mark interprets as being quiet and subtle in my presentation style.

If that's true, then how do I carefully communicate without coming across as a pussy? Damned if I know.

Sofie: I notice that when I avoid taking responsibility for what I am saying I also avoid eye contact with the person I'm talking to. The other day Emma said,

"If you want me to believe you, look me in the eye and say that again." Whoops, busted!

Richard: Very cool!

It's crucial that we own our messages. If we can't fully stand behind our words, the people we are addressing will, most likely, dismiss our messages as unimportant. And if we get pegged as someone who can't or won't take responsibility for our words and actions, we'll never be successful in establishing long-term relationships. It simply boils down to an issue of trust and authenticity.

Gretchen: I'm beginning to realize that if I just come out and say that I'm feeling jealous it doesn't hurt as bad as when I try to pretend I don't have or shouldn't have those feelings.

The same thing is true when I tell Eddie, "I feel jealous when this or that happens." It's so much better than saying, "When you do this or that it makes me jealous."

The thing I've discovered is it's not Eddie doing this or that that makes me jealous, it's me interpreting his actions through my insecurity and fear. I know this because I am certain he'd never do anything to purposefully hurt me... unless, of course, he has me tied to the bondage chair.

<Laughter>

Eddie: This is a pretty big breakthrough, huh? Gretchen and I talked about this very thing last night.

But I want to add something I was just thinking about. I could easily take a more active role in this too. So when Gretchen and I are discussing a subject that is sure to trigger her jealousy response, I could easily say something like, "In the past, when we would have this conversation, I know you felt threatened and insecure. If you feel that way again, I'll understand, but I believe we need to push through it this time, don't you?"

Gretchen: Oh yeah, that would be helpful. The more opportunities I have to own my shit rather than shirk it off on you, the better we both will be.

Richard: Let's recap, shall we?

A lot of what we've been talking about today can be boiled down to four simple principles of active listening. They are:

1. *Affirm content*
   - This may include maintaining eye contact and staying engaged by nodding in approval.
2. *Paraphrase the message*
   - By using phrases such as "I hear you saying," (here you summarize the of message) we confirm with the sender that we understand the message.
3. *Clarify the implicit*
   - Bring out the unspoken content (underlying meanings) and have the sender confirm (or not confirm) it. For example: "What did you mean when you said xyz?"
4. *Acknowledge the feelings as well as the message*
   - State that you understand the message, but also ratify the feelings that come with it. For example: *"Thank you for explaining how you feel when I am late for something important. I get it!"*

Let's take a short break. Stretch your legs, grab some refreshments, and we'll regroup in fifteen minutes.

My Check-In

Richard: What did the *Essentials of Effective Communication* exercise uncover for you about your Active Listening skills? What are your successes? Where do you need more help?

Richard: Our last area of concern for today is successful problem solving in kinky, BDSM, and alt relationships.

Even the strongest relationships go through periods of distress and turmoil. Disagreements, misunderstandings, and personal foibles can cause contention and conflict.

So let's see if we can come up with some practical tools and techniques to 1) handle common alt relationship-related issues, and 2) successfully navigate our relationship conflicts.

Exercise 2 – Tools and Techniques for Navigating Alt-Relationship Conflicts

Begin by jotting down a half dozen or so key words or phrases that identify the issues and problems you've encountered in your alt relationships. And then see if you can come up with a list of a half dozen or so key words or phrases that suggest possible solutions to those issues and problems.

Richard: Who wants to begin this round?

Stan: I was much more successful coming up with key words for my issues and problems than possible solutions. No surprise there, I suppose.

My list of issues: Need / Want / Expectations

My list of solutions: Be able to give before I expect to get

Gretchen helped me see that if I want something, the best way to get it is to make myself attractive to the person who is in a position to give me what I want. This advice is helping me reevaluate my entire approach to fulfilling my desires. Again, thank you Gretchen.

Gretchen: You're welcome again, Stan. I'm glad I was able to help.

My list of issues: Stress / Irritability / Bitchiness

My list of solutions: Get more sleep / Pamper myself

Stress and sleep deprivation make me irritable.

Eddie and I both have full-time jobs and a couple of our kids are having financial problems. So sometimes the stress of it all makes me a bitch on wheels. When I don't take care of myself and let my internal batteries run down, I set up the perfect conditions for a confrontation.

I also know that if I take time for myself—a long, luxurious bath or a massage—I calm down almost immediately. When I eliminate the stress, I feel more capable of being submissive and I'm also more pleasant and available to Eddie.

Sofie: I brought this up a little while ago, but it bears repeating. Where are the role models for healthy, integrated, alternative lifestyles?

My list of issues: Rushing to judgment / Insecurity / Knowing myself

My list of solutions: Fact-finding / Negotiation / Checking in with myself

Before I can negotiate for a solution to a problem with one of my partners, I need to know what's buggin' him or her. Sometimes I think I can read their mind and so I go off half-cocked. I try to jump ahead to the negotiation part, but if I didn't do my fact-finding first I only make matters worse.

Oh, and I should probably say that sometimes I get all bent out of shape about something, but I don't actually know what it is that's buggin' me. Like I've been known to fly into a rage, but upon closer inspection I realize I'm not angry, I'm scared. Or I could be upset at Caleb or Emma about some stupid crap, but upon closer inspection it's just that I'm all like PMSing.

What I'm trying to say is that unless I stop and try to pinpoint what's actually going on with me, I can't have a meaningful discussion with my partners about resolving whatever it is that buggin' me.

Has this happened to anyone else?

Seiko: I can identify with that, Sofie. Sometimes I'm too clever by half.

My limited forays into the scene are teaching me to be more patient and body-aware. Maybe, just maybe, my IQ is getting in the way of my learning some of the lessons that others seem to pick up with ease.

My list of issues: Letting go / Staying in the moment

My list of solutions: Sensuality / Patience

I'm hoping that, with time, I'll be able to improve my right brain functioning. I want to become more intuitive and holistic to balance my left-brain, analytical, and rational capabilities. But that's like learning another language, isn't it?

Eddie: Being the Master of our household is a lot of responsibility. It's not just my wellbeing that I need to concern myself with, there is also Gretchen and the likelihood of integrating another female slave into the family. These concerns were on my mind when I created my lists.

My list of issues: Decision maker / Authority / Consultation

My list of solutions: Protocols / Consensus

I know that the final authority for our structured M/s relationship falls to me. I'm good with that. However, I want Gretchen to know that I am interested and even dependent on her input. Despite the fact that we live our M/s relationship 24/7, strict protocols often make communication awkward, at least it does for me.

And when it comes to problem solving, I want my slaves to know that I'm not perfect and I don't always have the right answers. That's why I put consensus on my list of solutions.

Brodie: Every relationship has its bones of contention. I totally think it's natural and even healthy to want to hash things out. It's so much better to get things out in the open than to let them fester all bottled up inside.

My list of issues: Confrontation / Integrity / Speaking my mind

My list of solutions: Listen / Acknowledge / Defuse

Like I said awhile ago, I'm trying to adapt my style of dealing with a disagreement or an argument. I don't want things to just explode, letting words and feelings fly in every direction.

So now I'm practicing a different method whenever possible. I try to give my venting some structure. I try to listen and acknowledge feelings, both my own and the other person's, and I try to see if we can defuse the volatile situation with compromise.

I'm not always successful in this, not by a long shot, but I am dedicated to improving my success rate. And I think trying something is better than just thinking or talking about it.

Alicia: That's a great approach, Brodie. I can see the value in making the issue a problem to be solved rather than something to fight over. I had a lot of the same things in mind as I made my list.

My list of issues: Anger / Disappointment / Being heard

My list of solutions: Input / Cooling off / Synthesis

I work in IT (Internet Technology), and we at work have a mantra: "When troubleshooting, the rational approach is the only approach that will succeed." So I started to work some of that into my day-to-day relationship problem solving.

The most important part of my solutions strategy is the cooling off part. There's no room for rationality when things are at a boil.

Mark: I'll go next.

This is all pretty new to me, at least when it comes to my personal relationships. A lot of you guys are saying that you pull problem resolution strategies from your work life or your alt-culture life. I like that. I need to do that, too.

My list of issues: Impatience / Dismissive / Bulldozing

My list of solutions: Listening / Acknowledging / Resolving

Willie mentioned last week that we often fight about money. I mean, who doesn't, right? But when we fight we nearly come to blows. Some of this can be chalked up to testosterone, but I'm a belligerent asshole when I want to be.

However, I do know better because I couldn't get away with that kind of behavior at the office. But then again, I'm not so emotionally vulnerable at work as I am at home.

Hey, maybe I just hit on a solution! Funny how that happens. Maybe if I can step outside myself for a bit, ya know, kind of check my emotional baggage at the door sort of thing, maybe then our arguments won't be so volatile.

Blake: I'm picking up some very important common threads here. First, when our egos are involved, an argument can quickly spin out of control. Second, strategies from other parts of our life can be applied to our alt-culture problem solving.

My list of issues: Insecurity / Blaming / Retreating

My list of solutions: Share feelings / Non-confrontational / Compromise

I was thinking about the role of a safeword in a BDSM scene. I was thinking that if I applied that same principle to conflict resolution I'd always have a way to let my partner know when I feel threatened or when the confrontation is veering toward emotional violence.

Richard: Great points, all you guys. And yes, Blake, you are absolutely right. By using a safeword or simply just a timeout, you can let your partner know that you've reached your limit. It's actually a great technique I teach vanilla couples in my therapy practice. It's a vital part of fighting fair. Ideally, of course, the safeword ought to be introduced and agreed upon at some point before the discussion or argument.

Willie, you are next. What did you write down?

Willie: I like that, Richard. I gotta try that.

Being the last one to respond in this particular go around means that someone else has already mentioned most of my thoughts and insights. So excuse me if this sounds repetitive.

My list of issues: Being heard/ Resentment / Withdrawing

My list of solutions: Timing / Situation / Tone

My biggest concerns have always revolved around being heard or even noticed in my relationship.

You've heard Mark and me talk about our relationship woes both last week and earlier today. So I won't repeat that stuff now. What I will say is that just hearing us talk out loud about our problems has really been helpful.

When I feel like I'm invisible, I become filled with resentment and instead of dealing with it I withdraw. I've decided today that this has gotta stop. I'm going to attempt to solve my problems by timing my relationship discussions with Mark better. I'll no longer try to get him to listen to me right after he gets home from work. I want to create an environment where we can meet as equals, where I'm not so needy and he's not so distracted. I think maybe a planned weekly or biweekly check-in discussion might help. I figure if we consciously set aside a time and place for our relationship talks it'll send an important message—we're worth the time and effort and so is our relationship.

And finally, I plan to change my tone when talking to him about important stuff. He wants me to be more assertive so that I can compete with everything else that is going on in his head? Ok, I can do that.

This session has been a revelation. Thank you everyone, especially you, Mark.

Your Turn

Richard: What did the *Tools and Techniques for Navigating Alt-Relationship Conflicts* exercise uncover for you about your problem-solving skills? What are your successes? Where do you need more help?

Richard: Okay, you guys. That's it for today. But before we close, I want to walk you through this week's homework. It's a bit more challenging than last week. Hopefully, each of you will rise to the occasion.

AT-HOME WORK

Week 2 — An Inventory for Keeping Things Fresh and Interesting

Long-term relationships of any stripe are difficult to maintain; BDSM and kinky relationships are even more so. Here's an inventory of common pitfalls and some life-affirming antidotes to the periods of ennui and tedium we all encounter along the way.

Choose at least three of the six general categories below. Rate yourself on a scale of 1-5 (five being your best effort) on how well you are doing with each question in that category.

Familiarity Breeds Contempt

Are you taking your partner(s) for granted? Recent research shows that gratitude is associated with satisfaction and happiness in a relationship.

- Are you saying thank you often and sincerely?
- Are you grateful for the abstract things your partner does, like making you laugh?
- Can you express your gratitude even when in the middle of an argument?
- Communication is lubrication. Are you talking about your fantasies and desires with your partner(s)?
- Can you create an erotic map of your lives both individually and together? It'll make exploring and sharing your kinks and fetishes easier.

Break Up the Routine

The danger in every busy life is that our routine will become a rut. Ruts signal that we have become bored or, worse, lazy.

- Have your roles and protocols become stale and rote?
- When was the last time you broke your routine with a little spontaneity?
- Do you think romance is only for vanilla folks?
- Can you plan sex or play without it becoming a hindrance to passion?
- Has sex become a low priority?
- Have you updated your play-partner checklist of negotiable and hard limits? Consider playing Yes, No, or Maybe.

Mutual Satisfaction

Many newbies to the culture make the mistake of assuming power exchange is all about the Dominant, but submissives have fantasies and desires too.

- Is your D/s or M/s relationship all about mutual satisfaction and fulfillment?
- Does the dynamic in your power exchange flow from the bottom up to the top?

- Is your submission appreciated as a gift and respected accordingly?
- Is your D/s or M/s relationship caught up in culture-related trappings, but losing sight of the mental and emotional aspects of dominance and submission?

Fighting Fair

Some believe that arguing is a sign of incompatibility or an indication that the relationship is in trouble. Truth is, it's not the differences between partners that cause conflict, it's how they handle their differences.

- Is listening as important in your communication style as knowing how to express yourself clearly?
- Are your arguments about understanding or agreement? One is important; the other is not.
- Are you putting your partner on the defensive? If anger dominates your arguments, they will be unproductive.
- Do you argue to win or find a compromise?
- Are your arguments a safe space for airing differences?

Spend Some Time Apart

For some this seems counterintuitive, but as they say, absence makes the heart grow fonder. It also keeps long-term relationships interesting.

- Do you have private time and space for yourself every day?

- Do you have outside interests and friendships that enhance your relationship(s)?
- Do you provide your partner(s) space to nurture and develop interests that you may not share?
- Are your satellite relationships providing positive feedback for your primary relationship?

Discover Things Together

This is a great way to begin a relationship as well as reinvigorate a long-term relationship.

- Are you setting your alt-culture goals together? Do you know where you want to be in 1, 3, 5 years?
- Do you regularly reevaluate your protocols?
- When was the last time you added something new to your long-term alt relationship(s)?
- Are you flexing your mental muscles and using your imagination? Can you create an aura of dominance or submission by just the way you move, speak (or don't speak), and act?

"Having sex is like playing bridge. If you don't have a good partner, you'd better have a good hand."

Butch Hancock

Week 3

Thorns Among the Roses

Checking In & Workshop

Richard: Welcome back, everyone. Today marks the halfway point of our workshop. I'm really impressed with the momentum that's gotten us to this point, so let's keep it going, shall we?

This week our check-in and workshop segments will be combined. I want you to focus your attention on last week's at-home work exercise and what it brought up for you.

Since our homework for last week was pretty involved, I'd like to give today's check in a bit more structure. Besides, I know how much you guys like structure.

There were six general categories in the *Inventory for Keeping Things Fresh and Interesting.* You were invited to choose three of those categories and then respond to each question by rating yourself on a scale of 1-5 (5 being your best effort) on how well you are doing with each. Here's how I'd like the check-in to go. We will go through each category, one by one. Those of you who chose that category will walk us through each of your responses to the five questions in that category.

Let's begin with the first general category: **Familiarity Breeds Contempt**.

Did anyone choose this category?

Willie: I did! So I'll go first today, if that's ok.

I want to begin by saying that I really got into this exercise. It took me practically all week to work through each of the questions under each of the general categories. I know I was supposed to pick three, but they were all so interesting and insightful that I wanted to think about each and every one. I found myself writing volumes in my journal about the things that came to mind for me in each category.

Familiarity Breeds Contempt was the first category on my list. Here's how I rated myself in terms of the questions:

Are you saying thank you often and sincerely? I gave myself a 3. I'm sure I think I say thanks more often than I actually do. I mean, I think Mark knows that I'm grateful for everything he does for me, but that's the problem, isn't it? If I'm going on assumptions, maybe I'm not actually expressing myself like I should.

Are you grateful for the abstract things your partner does, like making you laugh? I gave myself a 4, but only because I am grateful most of the time. I'm just that kind of guy; I'm pretty upbeat and I think my life is pretty wonderful. But after the first question, I realize I could really improve on articulating my thanks.

Can you express your gratitude even when in the middle of an argument? I gave myself a 1. I suck at this, and not in a good way.

Communication is lubrication. Are you talking about your fantasies and desires with your partner(s)? I gave myself a 4. Mark and I like to talk about what and who gets us hard, the more explicit the better. I think it's a real turn on for us both.

Can you create an erotic map of your lives both individually and together? I never thought about doing anything like this before and I was all ready to give myself a 1 on this question. But then I thought, *That's not fair.* Just because I hadn't thought of doing it didn't mean I couldn't. It took me a couple of days, but I finally came up with *my* erotic map and *our* erotic map. This totally knocked me out. I think this was the coolest thing about the whole homework exercise. By the way, I gave myself a 5 for all my effort.

Alicia: Hi everyone! I'm so glad we're all back together again. I can't get over how much I was looking forward to today. I feel like we've bonded on some level and I couldn't wait to get back with you guys again.

Ok, so I chose the **Familiarity Breeds Contempt** category too, and like Willie, it was my first choice out of my three.

Here's how I rated myself:

Are you saying thank you often and sincerely? I gave myself a 4. Like you, Willie, I probably think I express my gratitude more often than I actually do. So I had to ask myself, would it really be all that difficult to make more of an effort? I think that if I were more expressive with my gratitude and spread it around a bit more freely, it would vastly improve the quality of life for all concerned.

Are you grateful for the abstract things your partner does, like making you laugh? I sure am! I gave myself a 4 on this one too.

Can you express your gratitude even when in the middle of an argument? I gave myself a 2. I sometimes say to myself, during an argument, *That makes sense.* Is that the same thing as being grateful? Hell, I don't know. But it does suggest that I'm at least paying attention.

Communication is lubrication. Are you talking about your fantasies and desires with your partner(s)? I only give myself a 2 here. I'm not sure why, but being expressive about my fantasies doesn't come easy to me. It's not that I don't have fantasies and desires; I do, and lots of them. I'll even share them if I'm asked, but I'm not one for volunteering that sort of thing.

Can you create an erotic map of your lives both individually and together? I gave myself a 3 on this one because I did a workshop about six months ago that used the concept of an erotic map as part of the presentation. Curiously enough, while I made a map of my own erotic life, I've never considered doing that for my erotic life with a partner. I need to get on that.

Hey Blake, let's give it a try.

Stan: I'll go next. The **Familiarity Breeds Contempt** category was my first choice too.

Here's how I rated myself:

Are you saying thank you often and sincerely? I gave myself a 1. Gratitude is not one of my strong suits. Some people, even some people who like me, have said I always have a chip on my shoulder. I think they're right. I know ya can't be grateful if ya think the world is out to get ya.

Are you grateful for the abstract things your partner does, like making you laugh? I don't have a partner at the moment, so I left this one blank.

Can you express your gratitude even when in the middle of an argument? Hell no! I gave myself a 1 on this, but if I could have given myself a 0 that would have been more honest.

Communication is lubrication. Are you talking about your fantasies and desires with your partner(s)? I had to give myself a 2 here because I try to do this with the dominant women I'm interested in. I'm like you, Alicia. I only share my interests if I'm asked. I never got the hang of volunteering that information or even soliciting it from someone else. I wonder, do you think that's a sign of shame?

Can you create an erotic map of your lives both individually and together? I gave myself another 1 on this. I've never heard of an erotic map before this exercise, but I suppose I see the value in it. That's it for me.

Richard: My bad! I took for granted that you'd be familiar with the concept of an erotic map when I created last week's homework. I apologize that I assumed too much.

To make a long story short, an erotic life map is exactly like a regular map only completely different.

<Laughter>

Just kidding.

An erotic map really is like a real map, only you focus on sexual things. It's a way of sketching out where you've been, where you currently are, and where you want to be in the future. Your erotic milestones—relationships, fetishes, protocols, and goals are all pertinent. As the homework suggested, if you have a sense of where you and your partner(s) have been and where you are now, you'll better understand how you might get to where you want to be individually and/ or together.

Like a street map, which will guide you to a physical destination, an erotic life map will guide you to a life fulfilled. However, a street map won't be able to tell you if any of the roads or highways you might want to travel are closed or blocked. The same is true of your erotic life map. Still, having a map will get you much closer to your desired destination than not having one at all.

Seiko: Thanks for explaining that, Richard. That's what I thought an erotic map was, but it's always nice to know for sure.

I chose the **Familiarity Breeds Contempt** category, but not as my first choice; it was my third. Here's how I rated myself:

Are you saying thank you often and sincerely? I gave myself a 4. It may be a cultural thing, but I was raised to say please and thank you, so I do it kind of automatically. I suppose I would have given myself a 5 on this if I wasn't concerned about the fact that maybe my automatic gratitude is not always that sincere.

Are you grateful for the abstract things your partner does, like making you laugh? I also gave myself a 4 on this one too. I am always telling Xiang thank you. But sometimes I think this gets on her nerves. Do you suppose a person could overdo this gratitude thing?

Can you express your gratitude even when in the middle of an argument? I didn't do so well on this one. I gave myself only a 2.

Communication is lubrication. Are you talking about your fantasies and desires with your partner(s)? I had to give myself a 1 here. I'm kind of shy when it comes to being vocal about my fantasies, especially if they involve Xiang.

Can you create an erotic map of your lives both individually and together? I left this one blank, because I didn't know what this meant. But now that I do, I think I could easily do this. Just between you and me though, there isn't a whole lot to map out. I'm just beginning my erotic journey.

Brodie: I included the **Familiarity Breeds Contempt** category as my second choice.

Are you saying thank you often and sincerely? I gave myself a 2. I think of myself as courteous, but it's often more perfunctory than sincere. I should probably work on that.

Are you grateful for the abstract things your partner does, like making you laugh? Like Stan, I don't currently have a partner, so I left that blank.

Can you express your gratitude even when in the middle of an argument? I'm really working on this.

Like I said last week, I'm trying to learn how to handle arguments and disagreements in a more rational, calm, and patient way. I try to express at least some gratitude during an argument, because it's a way of controlling my hostility. If I say something like, "Thank you for that," I'm less likely to blow my top. I'm not always successful, but it is a nifty strategy for keeping my temper in check.

Thing is, most of the time the person I'm arguing with thinks my gesture is insincere or I'm trying to be snide. But I suppose that's better than letting things boil over. I gave myself a 3 on this one.

Communication is lubrication. Are you talking about your fantasies and desires with your partner(s)? Oh yeah, big time! I had to give myself a 5. If I'm with a kinky partner, there's no end to the verbal mischief I can get into. And I love quizzing a partner about her fantasies. It's such a turn on. It makes for the best foreplay and we can do it almost anywhere.

Can you create an erotic map of your lives both individually and together? I didn't exactly know what this meant at first, but that didn't stop me from coming up with a pretty good guesstimate. And judging from what you said awhile ago, Richard, I wasn't far off the mark. I plan on making this a priority in the coming weeks.

Richard: The next general category is: **Break Up the Routine**.

Who chose that category?

Blake: I did. And here's how I rated myself:

Have your roles and protocols become stale and rote? I gave myself a 4 on this. Truth is, I'm still so new to all of this that there hasn't been enough time for me to get so comfortable in my scene play for any of this to become rote.

When was the last time you broke your routine with a little spontaneity? I gave myself a 2 on this one. As I've been saying over the last couple of weeks, I'm beginning to reevaluate my self-identification as a top. I don't know if it's fear of the unknown or just inertia, but this is much more challenging than I imagined it would be. Maybe that's why I'm looking for some encouragement and affirmation from you, Alicia.

Do you think romance is only for vanilla folks? No! I gave myself a 5 on this.

Can you plan sex or play without it becoming a hindrance to passion? I do really well with this too. Like I said a moment ago, the whole scene is still very new to me, so the excitement level is still always very high. And where there's excitement there's passion. At least that's so for me. Again, I ranked myself with a 5 on this one.

Has sex become a low priority? Are you kidding? No way! Sometimes I feel like a teenager. It's like boner city over here all the time. The interesting thing is that I have way more libido than I have outlet, if ya know what I mean. And therein lies the rub, no pun intended.

My horniness sometimes creates dangerous situations and opens the door to some poor choices. It's weird, because Alicia and I keep making the same mistakes, trying to make old, vanilla relationship rules apply to our newfound lives as kinksters. We really need to learn to break free of this. As a result, I didn't know how to rate myself on this question.

Have you updated your play-partner checklist of negotiable and hard limits? See, this is what I'm getting at. I think we... no wait, I mean *I* have a whole lot of work to do in this area.. I gave myself a 1 on this. My confusion about where I am on the top/bottom, Dom/sub spectrum is getting in the way of me growing and moving forward. After all, that's why I signed up for this workshop.

Hey, maybe I should be playing Yes, No, or Maybe with myself before I consider playing that with Alicia or anyone else for that matter.

Richard: There ya go! That's insightful. Good for you, Blake.

I firmly believe that the more we know ourselves, the richer our relationships will be. And we oughtn't fool ourselves into thinking that what we decide for ourselves in our youth will be equally applicable when we are older. It's simply not the case. The problem is there is precious little incentive, even in our alt culture, for creative self-evaluation and rediscovery.

As this exercise is showing us, being kinky doesn't make us immune to many of the problems that plague vanilla folks. In fact, some things in our alt culture militate against the very things that would keep our relationships fresh and vibrant. People can get so caught up in roles and protocols that it's like missing the forest because of all these damned trees.

Eddie: Isn't that the truth?

Gretchen and I have a bunch of kinky friends our age and older. We've known these people for what seems like ages. And we often remark about how staid things can become in long-term relationships even for us kinksters, or perhaps it's because we are kinky. Roles, like the ones we create for ourselves, can often be stultifying.

That's why I chose the category **Break Up the Routine** as first on my list. There's just so much about human nature that, if not kept in check, will produce tedium and boredom. Here's how I rated myself on these questions.

Have your roles and protocols become stale and rote? I gave myself a 4 on this.

I try to keep things interesting in our household. I'm stoked that Gretchen and I are finally able to live our M/s relationship 24/7. But I don't want to wake up one day and find that we are, like so many of our friends, just a couple of old fogies, Gretchen in her collar and me in my leathers slumped in our recliners bored stiff and unfulfilled. I'm the Master. I see it as my responsibility to keep things interesting.

When was the last time you broke your routine with a little spontaneity? I gave myself a 5 on this one. I pride myself on my ability to shake things up. My interest in incorporating another submissive woman into our household is exactly what I'm talking about. But I also don't want to be a jackass about the power I wield.

Do you think romance is only for vanilla folks? Not at all! I gave myself a 5 on this. Just because we kinksters do edgier stuff than our vanilla counterparts doesn't mean we're not being romantic. Like Gretchen is fond of saying, our M/s relationship, with its protocols and rules, says love and romance to us. And so does a flogger.

<Laughter>

Can you plan sex or play without it becoming a hindrance to passion? Oh yeah! Another 5 on this one. Gretchen and I learned a long time ago how to plan our play sessions in advance. When the kids were growing up everything had to work around their presence in the house, but we never let that get in the way of either the passion or the intensity.

Maybe we hit upon a secret. Those of us who have other responsibilities, like a family, revel in every opportunity to play, because the opportunities are often few and far between. Know what I mean?

Has sex become a low priority? I'm no longer a spring chicken with hormones raging. But nowadays I believe I have something even better. I have stamina. I used to go off half-cocked, if ya know what I mean. I never realized how disappointing that was to my female partners. Digging deeper into my Master role, over the last few years, has helped me learn to control my sexual response too. I told Gretchen just the other day, it's like I'm learning to top myself. Wait, I didn't tell you a number for this one. I gave myself a 4.

Have you updated your play-partner checklist of negotiable and hard limits? This is a really good idea and I need to get on that ASAP. I gave myself a 2 on this one.

Alicia: I'll go next. **Break Up The Routine** was my second category. And it pretty much follows after my first category, **Familiarity Breeds Contempt**, which I've already discussed. It's kind of like two sides of the same coin. Here's how I rated myself on these questions:

Have your roles and protocols become stale and rote? I wasn't sure how I should answer this. I know I'm in a state of flux in terms of my role and identity in the scene, so nothing is stale or rote about it. On the contrary, everything is up in the air. Actually, I'm hoping things will settle soon because I'm much better at life when I have a plan. I didn't give myself a number on this question.

When was the last time you broke your routine with a little spontaneity? I gave myself a 5 on this one. Like I just said, everything is fluctuating so I have yet to form a routine. This makes for some very interesting encounters. It's like I'm never quite sure if I'll be fish or fowl at any given time. Exciting? Yes, definitely! Anxiety-provoking? Oh yeah, that too!

Do you think romance is only for vanilla folks? No, I don't. Let me amend that. I would like a lot of romance in my life.

I don't think I'm being indiscreet when I say this, but Blake and I are really more fuck-buddies than lovers. You know, a "friends with benefits" sorta deal. We talk about this a lot. Will we decide to take our casual relationship to the next level? Who knows? I see potential; we're certainly compatible in a lot of ways. And I really liked your comment about a flogger being romantic, Eddie. I know exactly what you mean. Oh, and I didn't actually rate myself on this one either.

Can you plan sex or play without it becoming a hindrance to passion? Oh yeah! A 5 on this one.

I'm in an odd situation, at least as I compare myself with others. I prefer to keep my emotional relationships and my play relationships separate. My power exchange play is rarely about sex, at least not in terms of it being directed toward orgasm. I've been hearing much the same thing from others in the scene lately. I wonder, is that a trend?

Has sex become a low priority? I don't really know how to elaborate on this beyond what I've already said. I gave myself a 3.

Have you updated your play-partner checklist of negotiable and hard limits? In light of what you said awhile ago, Blake, I really need to revisit this whole thing with you. I want to be supportive and affirming of your discernment process. So when you're finished playing Yes, No, or Maybe by yourself, I want to play it *with* you.

Seiko: I'll go next!

Break Up The Routine was the second category on my list. Unlike Alicia, I thought this category preceded the **Familiarity Breeds Contempt** category, not followed after, as she has it. Maybe that's just splitting hairs, but that's how my mind works. This is how I rated myself on these questions:

Have your roles and protocols become stale and rote? No, I'm way too new to all of this to have had any of it become stale and rote. But as I said during our first session together a couple of weeks ago, I have real trouble seeing myself as a sub or bottom. I'm just guessing here, but I suppose if someone chooses one role over another because one role frightens her, then that's not much of what I like to call conscious decision-making. Does that make sense? I didn't rate myself with a number on this one.

When was the last time you broke your routine with a little spontaneity? I gave myself a 4 on this one. Heck, I can be spontaneous, just as long as I've planned it all out in advance.

<Laughter>

Do you think romance is only for vanilla folks? Like so many of you have already said, romance can be expressed in many ways. Some people want only roses. Others want only the thorns. I suppose wisdom comes from knowing which person is which. I gave myself a 4 on this one.

Can you plan sex or play without it becoming a hindrance to passion? I didn't know how to answer this question. I don't do a lot of initiating; I'm pretty passive. Maybe that's why Xiang taunts me about being a closet sub. By the way, is there even such a thing as a closet sub?

Has sex become a low priority? I'm afraid that I had to answer in the affirmative and gave myself a 2 on this one.

Let me explain. It's not that I want to be in this sexual wasteland, or at least I keep telling myself that. Truth is, I'm confused. I date men and tend to enjoy their company, but they don't turn me on, not like when I lived in New York. I'm beginning to see that it's Xiang that I am passionate about. But this is so hard for me to admit, it almost brings me to tears. I just don't know what to do with all my feelings for her.

See, I told myself I wouldn't cry and here I am crying.

I have nothing against lesbians, really. It's just that this is such unfamiliar territory for me. And I have no idea if Xiang feels the same way about me. I feel so weak and powerless, and out of control.

Have you updated your play-partner checklist of negotiable and hard limits? No, I haven't.

Willie: Maybe it's high time for you to have a little chat with Xiang, Seiko. How bad could it be? You might be pleasantly surprised. Sounds like there's a good chance Xiang would return your affections.

I remember when I started having feelings... sexual feelings for some of my homies in middle school. I thought, *Fuck me!* In the neighborhood where I grew up, that was a death sentence. I held it in as long as I could. Once out of high school, I began to experiment. Pretty soon I was sucking cock like crazy, all real on the down low of course. And, needless to say, I still couldn't self-identify. I was so ashamed and fearful. I was such a pussy.

After years of denial, I finally came around to accepting who I was. I simply couldn't stand the duplicity anymore. I started seeing this one guy I met in a park. After a few dates he took me to this leather bar in Manhattan. As soon as I stepped through the door, I knew I was a goner. A few months later—I was 26 then—I had one big coming out. Not only was I queer, but I was also a kinky, nappy-headed faggot.

That's got a nice ring to it, huh?

I can't help but laugh now, but the truth is that coming out kinky was as difficult as coming out as gay. I'm so glad that's all behind me.

Sorry, I got off on a little tangent there. Anyway, **Break Up the Routine** was the third category on my list. This is how I rated myself on these questions:

Have your roles and protocols become stale and rote? I gave myself a 2 on this one.

I do think I'm in a rut. You guys already know that neither Mark nor I are particularly comfortable bottoming or subbing for each other. I won't speak for him, but for me it's not like I have anything against being a bottom or a sub. On the contrary, I think it might be challenging to switch. But I don't give it up for Mark because of all the other relationship issues we have. The last thing I want to do is signal to him my surrender.

Sorry, hun, that just came pouring out of me. I hope I'm not embarrassing you, but now that the cat is out of the bag, so to speak, I see this as my truth.

When was the last time you broke your routine with a little spontaneity? I gave myself a 4 on this one.

Do you think romance is only for vanilla folks? I gave myself a 5 on this one. I am the consummate romantic.

Can you plan sex or play without it becoming a hindrance to passion? Another 5 on this one too. Mark and I have really weird schedules. Sometimes we can go days without spending more than an hour of being awake at the same time. We're really good at scheduling even the most routine things.

Has sex become a low priority? Oh hell no! I guess that's gotta be at least a 5, maybe even a 12.

<Laughter>

Have you updated your play-partner checklist of negotiable and hard limits? This is definitely on my to-do list. Maybe after this workshop the time will be right for taking a fresh look all this. I'm done!

Richard: The next general category is: **Mutual Satisfaction**.

Who choose that category?

Mark: Willie, you may be a kinky, nappy-headed faggot, but you will always be my kinky, nappy-headed faggot. And don't you ever forget it!

Thanks for being so honest. I think you and I suffer from much the same thing. And the fucked up thing is, I don't think either one of us equate being a bottom or a sub as weakness. But that surrender thing, that's some real shit, isn't it? That's why I'd like to go next, if that's ok.

Even though the **Mutual Satisfaction** category was my second choice, it gets to the heart of the problems Willie and I have.

When I did my homework last week, I breezed through this exercise. That's what I do when I couldn't care less about something; I simply go through the motions or blow it off completely. But after listening to all you guys being so straight, you should pardon the pun, with the group, I'm feeling more than a little sheepish. While you guys have been talking, I've been furtively changing the ratings I gave myself last week. This isn't gonna come easy, but maybe a little honesty will do me good.

Ok, here goes nothin'!

Is your D/s or M/s relationship all about mutual satisfaction and fulfillment? Last week I gave myself a 5 on this one. The more honest answer is a 1.

I was going lie to you like I so often lie to myself. I was going to say I'm all about mutual satisfaction. But that's bullshit. I am one selfish, self-centered mutherfucker. Here's how it's really is. As long as I get mine, just as long as I'm satisfied, the rest be damned. No wonder you don't want to signal surrender, Willie. I'd eat you alive. You know that. I know that, and now all these good people know that. Shame on me!

Does the dynamic in your power exchange flow from the bottom up to the top? I suppose that's how it's supposed to work, or work best. It certainly would signal something more egalitarian than what I'm used to. But truthfully, my self-interest doesn't allow for that. Don't get me wrong. If I'm punishing some willing sub, or fuckin' the bejesus out of some twisted power-bottom, it's a turn on to see him take everything I can dish out. But again, I don't think this is what this question is asking. My rating from last week was a 5. Today's rating is a 1.

Is your submission appreciated as a gift and respected accordingly? I don't do a whole of submitting. Next!

Is your D/s or M/s relationship caught up in culture-related trappings, but losing sight of the mental and emotional aspects of dominance and submission? Last week I gave myself another 5 on this. I sure was generous with the aces, huh?

Again, in all honesty, I'm way too vulnerable for this. That's why I'm like all swagger and bluster. I'm totally insecure on the inside. I've been like this since I was a kid. In fact, I can't think of the last time I allowed myself to be emotionally available. I see now how this has contaminated just about everything in my life, especially my relationship with you, Willie.

I feel wretched. I feel like people can see right through me.

Willie: Hey, come on, big guy.

Richard: Sometimes this exercise can get under a person's skin. Self-examination is hard, especially when we realize that we are coming up short.

While I'm glad you're being honest with yourself and us, Mark, I want you to know that we're here to build ourselves up, not run ourselves down. You've got things in your life that you're less than proud of? Fine, join the club. The object of this workshop is to discover strategies for improving what's not optimum.

You know, they say that confession is good for the soul. But I believe acknowledging our shortcomings is only good if it brings us to a change of heart, a change of mind, and a change in behavior. If confession doesn't do this, then it will only leave us, as you suggest, feeling wretched.

Buck up, my friend; we've all got things to work on. And take some solace in the fact that you are here, making an effort, right now, right along with the rest of us mere mortals.

Does anyone else have the **Mutual Satisfaction** category on their list?

Sofie: I do! By the way, thanks for that, Richard.

Can I tell a story? When I was a teenager I had terrible acne. I was so self-conscious about it that I learned to loathe myself. Every time a pimple would appear, I'd pick at it and pick at it in a vain attempt to rid myself of this curse. Of course, this would only make a horrible situation so much worse. In time my face cleared up, but unfortunately that cycle of self-criticism followed by acts of self-loathing and even self-harming persists in my life. Despite my veneer of self-confidence, there's a lonely, frightened, and pimply teenage girl just below the surface.

Whoops, did I say too much? See what I mean about my awkward internal teenager?

Anyway, the **Mutual Satisfaction** category was the third of my three categories. Here's how I rated myself on the questions:

Is your D/s or M/s relationship all about mutual satisfaction and fulfillment? My relationship with Caleb is veering in the direction of a D/s relationship, or at least I hope it is, but neither one of us has come right out and discussed it openly. This is pretty much par for the course. I guess I was thinking that maybe we'd both kind of slide into it and maybe discuss it later. But that is such a cowardly way of doing it, isn't it? I also see that this whole by-default thing, that I do so much of, is very unhealthy.

I think I mentioned at our first session together that both Caleb and I have some deep-seated trust issues we need to work out before we enter such an understanding. So, as a result, I didn't rate myself on this one.

Does the dynamic in your power exchange flow from the bottom up to the top? I had to giggle when I read this one. You see, Caleb has this total foot fetish thing going on. And when he gets his freak on I am treated to a good hour of foot worship. I am putty in his hands, if you know what I mean. So, in a very literal sense of the word, the "dynamic" does flow from bottom to top. I hope that counts, because I gave myself a 5.

<Laughter>

Is your submission appreciated as a gift and respected accordingly? I'm not the submissive in our relationship, but I truly appreciate Caleb's submissiveness. I gave myself a 5 on this one too.

Is your D/s or M/s relationship caught up in culture-related trappings, but losing sight of the mental and emotional aspects of dominance and submission? Not at all! We're nowhere near that kind of burnout. I didn't give myself a rating on this one.

Brodie: I'll go next. The **Mutual Satisfaction** category was my first category choice.

Is your D/s or M/s relationship all about mutual satisfaction and fulfillment? I gave myself a 4 on this. I probably would have given myself a 5, if I were in a permanent M/s relationship. But right now, my D/s connections are of a more casual nature. I like them well enough, but I long for something more enduring and permanent.

Does the dynamic in your power exchange flow from the bottom up to the top? Yes, I believe that it does. I know I'm more involved with a scene if my sub is really into it. Her submission feeds my dominance. I gave myself a 5.

Is your submission appreciated as a gift and respected accordingly? Like you, Sofie, I'm not a submissive, but I really appreciate and respect the submissives in my life. I mean, when you stop to think of it, there'd be no tops if there weren't bottoms and there certainly wouldn't be any Doms if there weren't any subs. So anyone who disrespects or devalues the person who provides them the opportunity to be fully who they really are, is a fool. I gave myself a 5 on this one too.

Is your D/s or M/s relationship caught up in culture-related trappings, but losing sight of the mental and emotional aspects of dominance and submission? I wish you could see my playroom. I confess I may have gone a wee bit mad with all my toys, but I defy anyone to tell me that a guy's kit isn't a part of his fetish. At the same time, I pride myself in keeping all the accoutrement in perspective. I certainly do have a fetish for toys, but it has yet to get the best of me. I'm confident that my gear isn't what makes me dominant. I suggest that dominance either comes from your soul or you're a poser. And no amount of toys would change that.

Oh right, my rating on this one is another 5.

Stan: The **Mutual Satisfaction** category was my second choice.

Is your D/s or M/s relationship all about mutual satisfaction and fulfillment? I didn't really know how to answer this, but I gave myself a 3 on this.

I've mostly been dependent on pro-Dommes for my scene play. I've grown very fond of two such women, but I'm certain the feelings aren't mutual. It's a business arrangement; I know that. But still, this is all I have, so it's precious to me nonetheless.

What tripped me up with this question were the words "satisfaction" and "fulfillment." I don't fool myself into thinking my pro connections are the real deal, but I do experience a deep sense of fulfillment when I get the opportunity to exercise my submissiveness. It's like I'm transformed. I'm calm and relaxed and I think I'm even a nicer person afterwards. Unfortunately, those feelings don't last, so real satisfaction is never achieved.

I don't know if I'm dating myself here or not, but I'm of the age when guys would get blue balls from being denied the sexual satisfaction we were so desperate for. Dating in my late teens and early twenties was like blue-ball city 24/7, if you catch my drift. I mention this because this is how I now feel about being a sub. It's like I can't get "laid" for the life of me and sometimes I actually ache from it.

Does the dynamic in your power exchange flow from the bottom up to the top? That's my experience, yes. But then again, I don't suppose there's any other way this would happen in a business arrangement, like the ones I have. I gave myself a 5.

Is your submission appreciated as a gift and respected accordingly? I'm going to be really cynical here and say the women I'm involved with work with me because it's their job. I am respectful toward them and I am generous with them, but am I appreciated? I don't know... maybe. I gave myself a 4 for my efforts.

Is your D/s or M/s relationship caught up in culture-related trappings, but losing sight of the mental and emotional aspects of dominance and submission? Oy, I should have such a problem!

The concept of culture-related trappings is like music to my ears. I practically swoon when I'm in a dungeon with one of my pro-Domme lady friends. I sometimes imagine myself going hog-wild with all the playthings that turn my crank. And ya know what? I could afford all kinds of excess. But I don't allow myself to go there; I deny myself that indulgence. I mean, having a houseful of underutilized toys, on top of all my unfulfilled urges and longings, would, I think, be too much for me to bear. You already know how desperate a man I am.

Blake: The **Mutual Satisfaction** category was my second choice too. And here's how I rated myself:

Is your D/s or M/s relationship all about mutual satisfaction and fulfillment? I gave myself a 4 on this. I guess there's always room for improvement, right?

I like to say I'm still evolving—top/bottom, Dom/sub, whatever. What I know for certain is that there's a lot of excitement involved in it all. I'm really getting off on the self-discovery aspect of it. I'm wondering if other people have experienced a similar awakening at any point in their lives. Or maybe most people recognize who and what they are from the get-go. If that's the case, it just seems to me that if one settles on all of this early in life, there's no room for growth or development later on in life. Maybe we could talk about this at some point.

Does the dynamic in your power exchange flow from the bottom up to the top? I never gave this much thought before this exercise. But now that I'm identifying less and less as a top, I see the importance of this particular power exchange dynamic. Wherever I wind up on the top/bottom and Dom/sub spectrum, I want to excel. That was my commitment to myself when Alicia and I launched into this. I went ahead and gave myself a 5.

Is your submission appreciated as a gift and respected accordingly? The very limited experience I've had so far in this regard has been very rewarding. Again, I have Alicia to thank for this. I don't think she knows this, but I think she's been very accommodating, supportive, and respectful of my evolution. I gave myself a 4.

Is your D/s or M/s relationship caught up in culture-related trappings, but losing sight of the mental and emotional aspects of dominance and submission? Luckily there's nothing like that in my life or in my relationship with Alicia. But I see where this could easily become a problem.

Sometimes I meet people at parties and I think to myself, *That person is all flash and no substance.* I wonder, is that a sign of boredom, or is that an indication that there wasn't much there to begin with? Anyhow, I'm good. Gave myself a 5 on this one too.

I'm done!

Richard: Ok, I'm gonna suggest that we take a short break. Stretch your legs, grab some refreshments and we'll regroup in fifteen minutes.

My Check-In

Richard: What did this exercise uncover for you? Did you choose any of these first three categories—**Familiarity Breeds Contempt**, **Break Up the Routine**, or **Mutual Satisfaction**? How did your rankings compare to your fellow group members? Did any of their discussion raise questions for you? Would you like to address any of the concerns raised by your fellow participants?

Richard: The next general category is: **Fighting Fair**.

Who choose that category?

Gretchen: Finally! I've been chomping at the bit for the opportunity to chime in. You'll pardon the mixed metaphor.

Seriously, I'm learning so much about myself by just listening to what the rest of you are saying about yourselves. I see a lot of myself, both the good and the disappointing in how you see yourselves and your relationships. Thank you for your honesty and I hope I can return the favor.

Although the **Fighting Fair** category was my third choice, I just had to jump in now because I'm about to burst. Here's how I rated myself on these questions:

Is listening as important in your communication style as knowing how to express yourself clearly? Honestly? And I'm talking about the big picture here, I really try my best at this, and give myself a 4.

When Eddie and I first got married I already had one fucked up marriage under my belt. I had learned how to hold a grudge like it had a handle. But I certainly didn't want to repeat the mistakes I made the first time around. The fact is, while I wasn't all that much the wiser back then, by the time we married we were beginning to dabble in BDSM. When we began to formalize our play into a M/s relationship, I was immediately comfortable in my slave role. That's pretty amazing, huh?

By the way, Blake, I wanted to say more about this when you raised the questions you did before the break. Maybe we can talk about chosen roles and evolving roles a bit later. At any rate, what I wanted to say is that my slave role helped me learn to listen better.

This attentiveness, particularly when we weren't involved in a scene, didn't come naturally. I remember struggling against this when we were first married, but somehow I hit on bringing my slave skill set into the skill set I needed to be a wife and mother. I don't know if I'm communicating this well or not, but those are the facts.

Are your arguments about understanding or agreement? I gave myself a 3 on this one. I guess sometimes I'm more successful with this than I am at other times. I kind of think the determining element is how important the subject matter is to me. Like when

Eddie and I are arguing about some stupid shit regarding how the house is run, I let him win.

<Laughter>

Just kidding!

Seriously though, I don't feel like I have to go to the mat every time we seem to be at cross-purposes. It's pretty easy for me to just let go and not pursue the issue.

Now, the same is not true when we are discussing (heatedly) something I'm truly invested in, or that pushes my insecurity buttons. The truth is that sometimes agreement isn't always possible. It's at this point that I want to learn how to better listen to understand as opposed to listen to agree.

Are you putting your partner on the defensive? I sure as hell know how to do that when I want to, but I don't think that's what the purpose of the question is.

I can be as manipulative as shit and I know it. I can say cruel things that not only hurt, but will also derail an argument. I try to maintain a handle on this as best as I can. Again, this is an instance where my slave skill set serves me very well. Without it I'd be this out-of-control bitch. I gave myself a 4 on this one, mostly because I try really hard.

Do you argue to win or find a compromise? I thought this question was just a variation on the second question about understanding and agreement, so I won't repeat myself.

Are your arguments a safe space for airing differences? I gave myself another 4 on this one.

Eddie and I really love one another. And I know this is going to sound trite and corny, but because of our deep emotional connection, we carefully avoid hurting one another. For example, I know for certain that if he were only concerned about his own desires he would have introduced another female sub into our household long ago. He hasn't done so, not because he is wavering on this, but because he is sensitive to me and my wellbeing. I love that about him.

That's why I'm diligently working on my jealousy and insecurity issues; like attending this workshop, for example. I want to reward him for his thoughtfulness and patience.

I'll get there soon, Sir, I promise.

Sofie: Hey Gretchen, if you could bottle some of that amazing goodness, and give some to me, I would put it to good use.

The **Fighting Fair** category was my first pick mainly because I'm clueless about it. Actually, that's not true. I pretty much know the difference between fighting fair and fighting dirty; I just don't apply what I know with my intimate partners. This is a consistent problem for me. I mean, how can I brag about being this total poly chick and disregard this fundamental aspect of healthy relationships? I suppose it all boils down to what I was saying earlier, before the break. Beneath my veneer of self-confidence, there's a lonely, frightened, and pimply teenage girl. So here's how I rated myself on these questions.

Is listening as important in your communication style as knowing how to express yourself clearly? Nope! Gave myself a 2.

While I absolutely expect my partners to listen to me, I'm not so good at showing them the same respect. Case in point, the other night Emma and I got into it AGAIN about my relationship with Caleb. I basically tuned her out because we've gone over this so many time my head hurts. All I was hearing was, *"Caleb... blah, blah, blah."* I was rolling my eyes at her in this total blow-off way, when she started crying. She said through her tears, "You didn't hear a word I said, did you?" Busted! It's true I hadn't. And get this; she was trying to tell me that she was rethinking her opposition to me seeing him. Damn, I felt so shitty. Not only because this was a really big moment for her, but also because if she'd done that to me I would have raised the roof with indignation.

I know it's a double standard and it's really unattractive, but there ya have it.

Are your arguments about understanding or agreement? Listen, the only reason my partners and I argue is because one or the other of them isn't in lock-step agreement with me.

<Laughter>

I gave myself a 2 on this one too.

Are you putting your partner on the defensive? Again, if that's what I have to do to "win" an argument, you bet I will. I rated myself with a 1 on this question.

Do you argue to win or find a compromise? Compromise? What's that?

Are your arguments a safe space for airing differences? Ahhh, not so much! I gave myself another 2 on this one.

I'd be pretty ashamed of myself right about now if it weren't for the fact that this exercise helped me see myself and my relationship dynamics for what I and they really are and not what I pretend they are. Now that I've done that I think I can make a change. I honestly believe that if I can see the problem in a non-threatening sort of way, I have a much better chance at making the necessary adjustments. And seeing that I'm the one who is confronting me with this, instead of either Emma or Caleb, maybe I'm on the road to recovery.

Can I read you the entry I made in my journal after I finished this exercise? Ok, so I wrote: "I'm ready for my next stage. I am ready to grow with my partners. I'm ready to make things happen. I'm ready to build relationships on a foundation of honesty and mutual respect. I'm ready to look deeper into myself and finally learn what I am capable of."

Willie: Very fuckin' cool, Sofie! You GO!

The **Fighting Fair** category was my second category pick. So here's how I rated myself on these questions.

Is listening as important in your communication style as knowing how to express yourself clearly? I probably would have given myself a 4, but I wound up giving myself only a 2. I downgraded my rating not for my listening capacity, which I think is pretty good, but because of the "express yourself clearly" part.

When I was doing this homework, I remembered last week's session and the comments that Mark made about my style of communication. Remember he said something like, "When he wants me to really be attentive to something he has to say, he should change his presentation style from his normal, quiet, subtle style to something that will get my attention." So ok, I'll own that. I know that's got to change, and I promise it will.

Are your arguments about understanding or agreement? I gave myself a 3 on this one.

Here's the thing. Arguments are a two-way street, right? And let's just say one person is trying to fight fair, but the other person isn't. How is that ever going to be a successful argument? Unless both people are coming at the argument with the same ground rules, I'm guessing that the argument will always sink to the lowest common denominator. Am I right or am I right?

Are you putting your partner on the defensive? I try not to. So I gave myself a 4 on this question.

But again, I was thinking back on what Mark said about my communication style last week. I thought to myself, *Oh my God, that's it.* I've been using my normal, quiet, subtle style so I wouldn't put him on the defensive, because, when someone is gettin' my face with bein' all bombastic I feel threatened. But apparently he isn't like me, and so all my efforts to avoid putting him on the defensive were actually being counterproductive. Go figure!

Do you argue to win or find a compromise? Jeez, I just don't know anymore.

Mark and I are very competitive, and I'm certain that our competitive personalities inevitably get all balled up in our arguments too. I mean, how could they not? I wound up giving myself a 2 on this one.

Are your arguments a safe space for airing differences? In light of how I answered the last question, probably not as frequently as I might like them to be. I gave myself another 2 on this one.

Mark: I'll go next.

The **Fighting Fair** category was my first category pick. If you think my ratings for the **Mutual Satisfaction** category were bad, hold onto your seat.

Is listening as important in your communication style as knowing how to express yourself clearly? I'm not a good listener; I know that about myself. In fact I even owned up to it in our first week's homework, the *Personality Characteristics Exercise.* Remember how I surprised the hell out of you, Willie, when I copped to this? I gave myself a 1 on this question.

Are your arguments about understanding or agreement? I gave myself a 1 on this one too. Hey, why isn't there a 0?

I'm all for arguments being about understanding, just as long as the understanding is that you agree with me.

<Laughter>

I know, I'm such a dick, right?

Are you putting your partner on the defensive? Listen, I'm a freakin' lawyer.

If putting my opponent on the defensive gets me the win, then that's what I'm gonna do. Gave myself a 1 on this question because this isn't about my work skill set, it's about my relationship skill set.

Do you argue to win or find a compromise? What do you think? Gave myself a 1 on this one too.

Are your arguments a safe space for airing differences? If you can go toe to toe with me and remain standing, then yeah, it's pretty safe to argue with me. If not, kiss your sweet ass goodbye. Guess what? Gave myself a 1.

This would be funny if it weren't so embarrassing.

Listen, I've decided to take to heart what you guys were telling me during the break. I was pretty low and your support and encouragement helped.

So ok, I didn't score very high on any of this stuff. But like you were sayin', Sofie, I can decide to grow the fuck up and at least make an effort to change. I'm sure you'd appreciate my commitment to be a more stand-up kinda guy, Willie. And I promise you, in the company of all these people, to do exactly that. Just as long as I can continue to be a domineering asshole in the courtroom, I think I'll survive. After all, I do have some standards to uphold.

<Laughter>

Brodie: It's funny that you should use the word domineering, Mark, because for the longest time, I thought domineering and dominance was much the same thing.

I'd like to share an embarrassing story, if you don't mind. About six months ago I was about to do this scene with this heavy-duty sub I was introduced to a few weeks earlier. She's nearly twenty years older than I am and has been in the culture practically longer than I have been alive. A mutual friend introduced us and I was pretty stoked that she even considered playing with me.

The time came for our play date, and I don't mind telling you that I was a bit intimidated at the prospect. I guess to compensate for my nervousness, I slipped into this bogus Dom persona that I used to use when I was fuckin' clueless about what I was doing. I think it was something I picked up from a porno movie when I was much younger. You see, I can get away with a fair amount of bluster and braggadocio because of my physical stature. So there I was swaggering around like this complete clown. It must have been insanely comical.

The woman was being much more patient than she should have been while I was performing these antics. In short order, however, she had had enough. Before we could get down to anything serious, she called me on my shit. "You know, dominance is something that you are; it's not something that you do. I think I can safely say that whatever it is that you think you are doing, it's not dominance." And with that, the scene was over. I was so humiliated, but I learned an important lesson.

I wonder, is this just a guy thing, or do novice fem-Dommes get called on this too?

Ok, the **Fighting Fair** category was my third category pick. Here's how I rated myself on these questions:

Is listening as important in your communication style as knowing how to express yourself clearly? I'm seriously working at it. I've been trying to learn how to deal with arguments and disagreements in a more rational, calm, and patient way. I know that when I get all riled up in the face of a confrontation, I rapidly lose control of the situation. And I don't want to lose control.

The lessons I learned in that bondage class, the ones I was telling you about, ya know breathing through my discomfort and anxiety before I react, are helping me with this. I gave myself only a 4.

Are your arguments about understanding or agreement? I gave myself another 4 on this one too. I think I have so much to learn, as evidenced by the story I just told, about how even a rebuke can be informative. But if I take the admonishment personally, then I'm not in any position to learn anything.

Are you putting your partner on the defensive? I hope not. Gave myself a 5 on this question.

Do you argue to win or find a compromise? I'd like to think I seek compromise, but frankly sometimes I don't see the value in my opponent's position. And even though I want to believe there is something worthwhile there, it doesn't mean the other person's position is right. I'm all over the board on this as you can see. Gave myself a 3 to show my ambivalence.

Are your arguments a safe space for airing differences? Again, if I feel there's value in my opponent's position, I will listen. I suppose that means it's a safe space. Gave myself 3 because I'm not sure.

That's it for me.

Richard: Ok, we're down to our last two categories. Who chose **Spend Some Time Apart**?

Eddie: Gretchen and I discovered that we both had this category on each of our lists. Hey, you want to share our ratings together, babe? By the way, this was my third category choice.

Gretchen: That works for me! **Spend Some Time Apart** was my first category choice.

Do you have private time and space for yourself every day? I wouldn't say that it happens every day, but I think we both know the value of privacy, right Sir? I gave myself a 4.

Eddie: I gave myself a 4 too. And, yeah, I think we both respect one another's privacy. She likes to read. I like to tinker in the basement. It's all good!

Gretchen: *Do you have outside interests and friendships that enhance your relationship(s)?* Yes, like Eddie just said, he's got his workshop and I have my books. We also have friends we socialize with independently. I gave myself a 4 on this one.

Eddie: I gave myself a 5.

Gretchen: *Do you provide your partner(s) space to nurture and develop interests that you may not share?* This one was a little tricky for me. I'm fine with Eddie spending as much time as he'd like in his workshop. For one thing, you should see the ridiculously cruel stuff he comes up with down there. He's like some mad scientist. I get wet every time he says, "Would you like to see what I just made?" And he can go out with the boys all he wants. The rub comes when he shows an interest in another woman, especially another submissive. Then I see red! I wish I could say that he's free to develop friendships, or, god forbid, sexual relationships outside our marriage, but as you know, I haven't been able to go there yet. Gave myself a 2.

Eddie: I think you know that my patience is running out on this, right? I think you know that I will push this to where I believe it is supposed to go, not just for me, but for you too. At least that's what I heard you saying right after the break.

Here's what's going to happen. I will invite another submissive to our family. This will happen sooner rather than later. I encourage you to join me in choosing someone who will be compatible with us both. But, I think you know that in the end, the decision will be mine.

I've wanted to say that to you as clearly as I just did for a very long time. Let our new friends here be witnesses. I rated myself with a 5.

Gretchen: Yes, thank you for speaking so clearly. Thank you for being so honest. I know you have our best interest at heart. Thank you for all your patience. I submit to your will, Sir.

The next question is: *Are your satellite relationships providing positive feedback for your primary relationship?* This might sound funny coming right after that little exchange, but I secretly believe that what will come next in our M/s relationship will nurture us both. I'm pretty sure that my resistance is just part of the baggage I've carried over from my old life script. But I will. I gave myself a 3 on this, but I'm pretty confident that this will be a 5 very soon.

Eddie: That's what I like to hear. Hold my hand and I will take you there. I gave myself a 5.

Seiko: Wow, that was very powerful, you guys. Thank you for sharing that with us.

Spend Some Time Apart was my first category choice, although I'm not really in a relationship. I suppose I'm technically in a relationship with Xiang. I mean we live together, but it's not an exclusive relationship. We both date and play with men. Yet I feel such a deep connection with her. In many ways, she is my mentor. I look up to her. And god knows, I get on her nerves. It's like I'm going all lezzie over here.

I can't figure out what to do next. Am I just supposed to come right out and tell her what's going on with me? I kind of think she knows already. I mean how could she not? I get all doe-eyed around her and act like some kind of love-struck schoolgirl. It's so embarrassing, but I can't seem to help myself.

And then there's the whole D/s thing. What am I supposed to do with that? As much as it freaks me out to say this, I know I'm a sub to her Domme even though we've not acted on that yet.

And all of this is completely out of character for me. I am in senior management at work. I have more than a dozen highly qualified people who report to me and I run rings around all of them, but at home I'm like this puppy. Sometimes the transition from my work life to home life gives me whiplash.

Ok, that's enough. This is how I rated myself on the questions in this category:

Do you have private time and space for yourself every day? Yes, a great deal of private time and space for us both. So much so that I'm never sure there's a real emotional relationship there. Maybe we're just roommates and one of us, me, has a crush on the other.

God, it's awful to consider that all my intense feelings could be dismissed in such a casual way, but I guess it's possible I'm nothing more to her than a roommate. I gave myself a 5.

Do you have outside interests and friendships that enhance your relationship(s)? Again the relationship thing! Maybe if I had a better sense of who we are together, you know like what the actual dynamic between us is, then I'd know how to answer this better. I gave myself a 2.

Do you provide your partner(s) space to nurture and develop interests that you may not share? More confusion! Truth is, I have more space than I have connection. I gave myself another 2.

Are your satellite relationships providing positive feedback for your primary relationship? For me, our satellite relationships, especially our connections with men, confuse me rather than provide positive feedback. I'm failing at this, aren't I? I hate to fail! Once in college I got a B+ instead of an A in a language course and I nearly came apart. It was the one and only time I got a less than A grade in all of my years in school. It was devastating.

As I'm saying this, I'm beginning to realize that my confusion about my relationship with Xiang is like getting that B+. I guess if I want an A, I have some homework to do, right?

Sofie: Honey, you got it bad and that ain't good! We should have a talk. You know what they say: "Once you go lezzie you never go back."

<Laughter>

For years I dated only women. I never had a problem self-identifying as a dyke. Then guys began to interest me and it was like pulling teeth to finally come out as bi. Most of my women buds freaked the fuck out! You have no idea how many friends I lost over this. But hey, it's all about honesty, right?

Emma hung in there though, god bless her. But I know that the Caleb thing is a constant irritant to her. She'll get over it.

Spend Some Time Apart was my second category choice. And these questions really helped me figure out a lot of stuff that had been pretty murky before this exercise. So here's how I rated myself:

Do you have private time and space for yourself every day? Oh yeah, I don't live with either of my lovers. I actually prefer it that way. The last thing I want is to be swallowed up by someone else's life. I gave myself a 5.

Do you have outside interests and friendships that enhance your relationship(s)? I do! I gave myself another 5.

Do you provide your partner(s) space to nurture and develop interests that you may not share? I do, but the curious thing is that both Emma and Caleb would rather have less space. Both of them want me to move in with them. But like I said, I don't want to be swallowed up by either of them. And I know that would happen given half a chance. I also know that both Caleb and Emma would feel like they won the tug-of-war for me if I relented and moved in with either of them.

At the same time, I sense that neither one of my lovers is prepared to give their all, because they interpret my living on my own as my being unable to commit. Which is like total bullshit, if ya ask me. Ya know, sometimes poly isn't such a picnic.

Then I remembered back to last week's discussion and I realized that a lot of this is my fault. I suck at communication and setting boundaries. If I were to be more forthcoming about what I *want* from them and what I'm prepared to *give* to them, perhaps we'd all get along better than we do. I gave myself a 2 on this one.

Are your satellite relationships providing positive feedback for your primary relationship? I have to say no. If I'm totally honest with myself, I'd have to say that neither one of my relationships feels like a primary relationship. Sure, I've been with Emma for way longer than I've been with Caleb, but my connection with Caleb is so much more intense. I mean, I can be a kinky little bitch with Caleb, but that would never cross my mind in terms of my relationship with Emma. I mean, is that even healthy? Can one turn this kinky stuff on and off like I seem to do?

And on top of all of this ambivalence on my part, I'm certain that neither Caleb nor Emma is feeling all that comfortable, let alone providing positive feedback for my relationship with the other.

I told myself I wasn't going to cry, but I can't help it. I've been so self-centered and I see that now. And I'm frightened that one or the other of these dear sweet people, who have been so patient with me, will just want to call it quits before I have the opportunity to mend the fences.

Oh, and I gave myself a 1.

Blake: Are you done, Sofie? Ok, then I'll go next.

Spend Some Time Apart was my third category choice, so here goes.

Do you have private time and space for yourself every day? I'm feeling more and more like you, Seiko. I'm not sure I know what's up with Alicia and me. We're certainly not a traditional couple in any sense of that word, but there's no denying we have a shit-load of chemistry, so much so that we both get really territorial about the other. At first, I thought this must be a sign of our love for one another. But then I thought, *Well if that's the case, how come we don't make an effort to articulate what it is that we're doing together?* And like you and your partners, Sofie, Alicia and I don't live together. And then I think, *Why the fuck not?* We hardly spend a night alone. Either she's at my place or I'm at hers. So what gives?

This exercise really raised more questions than it answered. I guess the short answer to this particular question is yeah, we allow for each other to have private time and space, but we rarely take advantage of it. So what does that mean? Beats the hell out of me. I gave myself a 3 mostly because I'm confused.

Do you have outside interests and friendships that enhance your relationship(s)? I do and she does. So I guess the answer is yes. I gave myself 4.

Do you provide your partner(s) space to nurture and develop interests that you may not share? Again, the answer is, I guess so.

We've never really sat down and talked about it in those terms. One thing I know for sure is that we love learning together. We do lots of hands-on classes and go to as many demos as we can. We're always so jazzed about these experiences that we can talk about them for hours afterward.

I know that doesn't really answer the question, but that's what we do. I gave myself another 4.

Are your satellite relationships providing positive feedback for your primary relationship? This is where things are the least clear for me.

To be perfectly frank, there's a great deal of inertia in our relationship. I mean, we seem to just let ourselves be swept along with the tide, without saying one thing or another about who we are to each other. Before this workshop, I kind of thought this was an indication that Alicia and I are really tight, but that's assuming a whole lot, isn't it? Which gets me back to how territorial we are about one another. I'm beginning to see that this makes no sense at all.

The fact is that we only pay lip service to the notion that we have this hip, open relationship thing going on. But both of us have flipped out when we felt threatened by something the other was doing or had done with someone else. And that's not right. I gave myself a 2.

Richard: Our last category is **Discover New Things Together**.

Alicia: If it's ok, I'd like to go next. The **Discover New Things Together** category was my third choice. But after listening to you, Blake, just now, I realize I should have made this my first choice.

Before I disclose how I rated myself on the questions in this category, I'd like to address some of the concerns that you raised in responding to the questions in your last category.

The first thing I want to say is that it was really uncomfortable sitting here listening to you talk about some of the intimate details of our life together. I hasten to add that my discomfort was not the bad kind of unease, but rather the good kind. Let me see if I can explain. I decided to do this workshop so I could pick up some tips on how to form and deepen my kinky relationships, especially my primary relationship with you, Blake. Yes, I do consider you my primary relationship. And if the truth were known, you are my *only* real relationship.

It was really hard for me to hear you describe our relationship using the word inertia, but you are absolutely correct. And I take responsibility for that right along with you. We've really let things slip, haven't we? There is no excuse for this laxity, but in our defense, I think there are several reasons why this has happened.

This workshop has really opened my eyes to what's been happening between us over the last few months. Last week's session, in particular, offered me my first opportunity to address the shift in the D/s dynamic in our relationship. That was huge for me. I felt empowered talking about myself in dominant terms. And I sensed that you are getting pretty comfortable with your developing submissive self. This week's session has also been helpful in as much as I'm seeing patterns, both good and bad, in how I involve myself with people that need some adjusting.

I guess what I'm trying to say is, I hear you. I hear your distress and confusion. I want to work with you on making what we have better and richer for us both. Maybe now that we have a clearer sense of who each of us is, maybe we'll be more successful in articulating who we want to become as a couple. Maybe that doesn't have to be a monogamous or exclusive relationship, but I can't picture my life without you. I want you to know that I'm open to discussing all the options, everything from just casual fuck buddies and play partners to a committed long-term D/s or even M/s relationship. Let's make this happen together, ok?

Wow! I suppose I could have saved that for our ride home, but I felt such urgency in what you were saying, Blake, and I wanted the other group members to hear what I had to say. I hope that wasn't too awkward for you or anyone else. On to my rating on these category questions.

Are you setting your alt-culture goals together? Do you know where you want to be in 1, 3, 5 years? I gave myself a 1 on this question. And just so you know, the reason I gave myself such a low ranking on this is I wasn't anymore sure of what was going on with Blake and me than he was of us. I think if you ask either one of us this question in a month we will both score a 5.

Do you regularly reevaluate your alt-culture protocols? This workshop has opened the door to that happening for us... I mean me. Ya know, I hope I can do this workshop again in like a year. I have a sense that I will be a completely different person by then.

When was the last time you added something new to your long-term alt relationship(s)? I couldn't rate myself on this because I'm not in a long-term relationship... yet.

Are you flexing your mental muscles and using your imagination? Can you create an aura of dominance or submission by just the way you move, speak (or don't speak), and act? I gave myself a 2 on this, but I have yet to begin to really blossom along these lines. All I can say is look out in the future because I expect great things from myself and I generally don't disappoint myself.

That's it for me.

Stan: Ya know, I almost didn't come back to the group after the first week. In fact, I wanted to leave at the break that first week. I felt so out of place. You all seemed so confident and comfortable in who you were and how you were getting on with your life. And I felt like such a klutz. I was embarrassed and ashamed when I had to recount all my social faux pas. I wanted to run and hide and never think about any of this ever again.

While it might not be obvious to anyone else, I am my own worst critic. My prickly exterior aside, I am frustrated and discouraged by my inadequacies. It seems the harder I tried to compensate for my shortcomings, the more awkward I became. I can't win for losing. I'm not sure why I kept coming back to the group. I guess I'm just a glutton for punishment. Good thing I identify as a submissive, huh?

<Laughter>

But I'm really happy I stuck it out. Now that I've had a chance to see you guys as you really are, with all your insecurities and relationship problems, I don't feel so awkward myself. Let's face it; you're fucked up, just like me.

Ok, maybe not as bad as me, but still I have to tell you, I take a perverse kind of comfort in that.

Now that I feel a little more at ease with you guys, I hope you don't mind if I get some things off my chest. Part of my problem has always been my unwillingness to reveal my insecurities. I was bullied as a kid and I hated myself for it. Weakness of any sort terrified and sickened me. So I learned early on that the best defense is a good offense. Whenever I was faced with a threatening situation, I increased the bravado, as a kind of distraction, and somehow I'd squeak by. This soon became a way of life. By the time I was in high school, I was the one dishing out the abuse. Soon I didn't have to be afraid anymore, but everyone else did. I did some unspeakable things, things that I'm now deeply ashamed of, but at the time, I thought they were necessary to keep up the façade.

Unfortunately, all of this had other undesirable consequences. Being a bully stymied my submissive sexual interests. I didn't know how to do both, ya know, how to be a sub and Master of the Universe at the same time.

As you already know I have no submissive skills to speak of. Until now, I was too afraid to ask for help because it showed my inner weakness. I'll be the first to admit that I have a very long way to go before I achieve my alt-culture goals, but at least now I feel part of a community of others trying to get their shit together.

Discover New Things Together was my third category choice. Let me just cut to the chase. I gave myself a 1 on all the questions, so I won't belabor this by going through each of the questions separately.

Mark: So is that why you're being such a dick about the gays?

Stan: 'Fraid so!

Mark: Well, at least you're being honest.

I wanted to jump in your shit the first week of this group. It took all my self-restraint not to lay you out. But now I see that you and I are a lot alike. We suffer from the same insecurities and we've built up the same kind of defenses. Your homophobia is external and mine, I regret to say, is internal. It's no accident that I can't bottom or sub, even for Willie. And when I top its really aggression and not eroticism.

Weakness of any sort, even perceived weakness in others, like the way they handle themselves in a tight situation, makes me sick inside. I know that you've already discovered this about me, Willie. And that's probably why you were so insistent that we do this workshop together. I know you've been hoping that I'd finally face this because our marriage hangs in the balance.

I've never said any of this aloud before, although it has been a constant, never-ending pounding in my head since I was a snot-nosed kid. My terrible secret has crushed all the kindness, gentleness, and compassion out of me so I tend to seek out those qualities in other men. Unfortunately, as soon as I begin to interpret these qualities as weakness in the other person, it signals the end of the relationship. I am both drawn to and repulsed by the same things. How fucked up is that?

All right, let me get to the questions for the **Discover New Things Together** category. By the way, this was my third category choice. Like for the last two categories, I've tossed the ratings I gave myself last week and will rate myself more honestly now.

Are you setting your alt-culture goals together? Do you know where you want to be in 1, 3, 5 years? I have to give myself a 1 on this question. What I know for certain is that I want to start doing this in earnest, with Willie. And I want to start from a more honest place. So hopefully it's not too late and I'll be able to pull my sorry ass out of the fire.

Do you regularly reevaluate your alt-culture protocols? Like you said, Alicia, this workshop has provided me an opportunity to take a fresh look at myself. And who knows where that will lead.

When was the last time you added something new to your long-term alt relationship(s)? Do bombshells count? Good! Then the answer is TODAY!

Are you flexing your mental muscles and using your imagination? Can you create an aura of dominance or submission by just the way you move, speak (or don't speak), and act? Last week I gave myself a 5. And to some degree, that still holds true now. I've been told I cut an imposing figure in my leathers. And that hasn't changed. Maybe from now on though, I'll be able to act from a position of strength instead of fear and my play will reflect my eroticism instead of my rage. We'll see.

Gretchen: Damn! You guys are a hard act to follow. I'm going to guess that being this forthcoming in such a public forum must be really exhausting. I know I'm drained and I was just a bystander. There's something about this kind of raw humanity that is both compelling and scary, and cleansing too I would guess.

You know, Mark I never thought a gay person could be homophobic. But I see the wisdom in what you just said about yourself. Thank you for that; it opened my eyes.

Eddie and I both chose this category too. It was our second choice for both of us. We'd like to respond together, like we did with the last category.

Are you setting your alt-culture goals together? Do you know where you want to be in 1, 3, 5 years? I gave myself a 4 on this question. Eddie and I have always been in sync with where we want to take our M/s life together. That is, up until we began to discuss the addition of another sub to the mix. I've always trusted Eddie and, despite my issues and uncertainty about how this will play itself out, I won't break that bond of trust with him now.

Eddie: I gave myself a 5 on this one.

I've never hidden my designs from Gretchen. This is uncharted territory for us both. There's a 50/50 chance that this could blow up in our faces, but we've weathered considerably heavier seas than this. And I'm confident that if we do this together, it will be enriching for us both, even if it doesn't work out.

Next question: *Do you regularly reevaluate your alt-culture protocols?* Yes, absolutely, particularly now that the kids have abandoned the nest. We've amped it up to a 24/7 thing and that's taken some adjustments to how we did our M/s in the past.

Gretchen: Yes, that's how I see it too. I don't see how people could manage a life transition like what we are doing without a regular reevaluation and the corresponding tweaking to stay on course. I gave myself a 5 too.

Next question: *When was the last time you added something new to your long-term alt relationship(s)?* I'm happy to report that rarely a week goes by without something new added to our life.

We love our toys, and Eddie's sinister brain has produced some stunning surprises, both literally and figuratively. I'm responsible for keeping us up to date on what's happening in the community. I'm kind of like the social secretary. I'm also the costumer and dresser. My responsibilities include boot blacking as well as sewing and mending. I take great pride in turning out my Master for every occasion. And I often have a few surprises up my sleeve too. I gave myself a 5 on this question.

Eddie: The reason I'm so creative with the toys and gear is that Gretchen is so game for experimentation. Her "can-do" attitude spurs me on to higher heights. I guess we both like surprises, so keeping things fresh and exciting isn't much of a challenge for either of us. I also gave myself a 5.

The final question in this category is: *Are you flexing your mental muscles and using your imagination? Can you create an aura of dominance or submission by just the way you move, speak (or don't speak), and act?* I gave myself another 5. I shine at this. And if you don't believe me, ask Gretchen. Ok, so maybe she'd be biased. But honestly, in my book the fewer the words the better. If I can't cast a spell without verbalizing my wishes, I'm not much of a Master.

Gretchen: I agree with Eddie. And if I can't express my submission without words, I'm not much of a slave. And I also gave myself a 5.

We know a lot of people in the culture, and we've seen some pretty silly stuff over the years. I think I can speak for both Eddie and me when I say the thing that makes us cringe the most is a showy Master/Dom and/or slave/submissive. Maybe it's just us, but that kind of display, you know, the kind of stuff you see in mainstream porn, not only smacks of the rank amateur, but also perpetuates an unhealthy and unrealistic stereotype. And stereotypes do nothing to advance the dominant culture's understanding of who we are and how we play.

Eddie and I are aficionados of the scene. We take who we are and what we do very seriously, but we never lose sight of the play aspects of it all. Our 24/7 M/s life together is like living a full-time fantasy for us both. It nourishes us, it gives us focus, it binds us together, and I think it makes us whole.

My Turn

Richard: What did this exercise uncover for you? Did you choose any of these last three categories—**Fighting Fair, Spend Some Time Apart,** or **Discover New Things Together**? How did your rankings compare to your fellow group members? Did any of their discussion raise questions for you? Would you like to address any of the concerns raised by your fellow participants?

Richard: Brilliant work today, you guys. I am so impressed.

But before we close, I want to walk you through this week's at-home work.

As you know, next week will be our final week together. It will also be the culmination of the process we began three weeks ago. We will be welcoming five extraordinary people to the group next week. They are the panel of skilled practitioners I promised you at the beginning of this workshop.

What will make this experience unique is that you will be asking all the questions and directing the discussion. Every time I have one of these panels the output is different because the questions that the panelists receive reflect the interests of that particular workshop's participants.

So it's up to you to make next week's discussion reflect your specific interests. And that's where your homework comes in.

To better prepare you for next week, I put together a thumbnail sketch of each of the panelists. In turn, and with your permission, I will also send the panelists a thumbnail sketch of each of you. I will crib these notes from your intake forms. But of course, you will also have time to meet and greet the panelists before the workshop begins next week. So I encourage you to get here early.

AT-HOME WORK

Week 3 — Questions for the Panelists

We've touched on several important issues in this workshop—communication, power exchange, polyamory, jealousy, sex and intimacy, relationship concerns, and conflict resolution among them.

Next week you will be joined by a panel of five skilled practitioners, reflecting an array of life experience, alt-culture involvement, and gender and race. They will be here at your disposal so I want you to make our time together worthy of their enormous generosity.

Please come prepared with at least five questions that reflect your interests, issues, and concerns.

I'd like to offer you a sneak preview of our panelists. These thumbnail sketches will help you formulate your questions. Feel free to direct your questions to a particular panelist.

....

Samantha is a bisexual switch who has been a part of the S/M and swinger communities for twelve years. Her favorite motto, which she uses for both worlds, is "If it isn't fun, then why the fuck do it?"

Following in a tradition of her own creation, she would never claim to know the One True Way. And she would not spend much time (let alone play) with anyone who would say such things.

She is an active volunteer and she has several causes (kinky and not) that she supports.

....

Lance Navarro is a performer in gay porn. Over the course of his porn career, he has been cast in many different roles primarily as a fisting bottom, but has also done sounding (urethral play), bondage (primarily as a sub), and played the Dom role in a few scenes as well.

He is also a masseur and sex worker.

He is polyamorous with two male partners. They all live in San Francisco, but live separately from each other.

His kink interests tend to come out more in his work, both with clients and in porn. He finds bondage and sensory deprivation to be especially useful with some of his clients. He also has a few clients that are into fisting and sounding. He is as skilled as a top and teacher as he is as a bottom. Spanking and flogging also interest him.

Lance is not currently active in any fetish clubs or organizations, although he regularly participates in various events and workshops.

He is a leather titleholder (Mr. Bolt Sacramento 2011) and competed at the International Mr. Leather Contest in Chicago. He is a frequent volunteer at St. James Infirmary, a clinic in San Francisco for current and former sex workers. It provides testing, counseling, and other services.

He also is a rider in the AIDS Lifecycle, a seven-day, 545-mile bike ride from SF to LA. He and has been for the last five years.

....

Byrdie is currently a student who is trying to find ways to recover from codependency in every aspect of her life, including romantic relationships, friendships, and work. She says she is learning to tell the difference between her instincts and knee-jerk reactions to triggers. She's also learning not to be so afraid of failure. As she says, she has just as much right to ask for things, speak out, act, and follow her dreams as anyone else.

Years ago, and despite her explicitly stated lack of interest in BDSM, friends persuaded her to experiment. This led to her first flogging, which she says she found both odd and pleasant.

Byrdie now says she is a hedonist. She wants what she wants when she wants it. She prefers primal play (punching, biting, scratching, growling) and deep thud sensations. And she has a fondness for Daddy/girl play.

She identifies as someplace between bisexual, pansexual, and heteroflexible, and is working to improve trust and sensual intimacy with other women.

She is one of the earliest members of the Wet Spot, now the Center for Sex Positive Culture. She is an avid attendee at culture-oriented workshops and is easing back into the social scene.

A four-year kink relationship that had D/s elements was the inspiration for her undergoing therapy to recover from codependence.

Most recently, Byrdie initiated the Seattle edition of Mollena Williams' *Know Your Negro,* a photography project intended to bring attention to the dearth of brown faces in the kink/Leather world.

....

Jack Slash, aka Jack the Journeyman, has been a member of the Seattle Leather community since 1982, and a practitioner of S/M since 1974. Before the year 2002, he was known as Dragon Xcalibur.

He holds two past Leather titles: Seattle Leatherwoman 1988 and Seattle Leather Ambassador 1997. In the eighties and nineties, he was a member of the now-disbanded Leather doo-wop singing group, the Sluts from Hell.

He teaches workshops, judges local and international contests on the West Coast, participates in local fund-raisers, and has led spirituality circles at Queer Leather events since the 1980s in Seattle, Portland, Vancouver, B.C., and San Francisco. Workshop presentations include blood sports, branding, impact play, fear and terror, ritual sacrifice, and honeybees.

He is a sought-after speaker on the topic of S/M and gender fluidity within the Leather community. As part of a group of community elders, he often shares his perspective on Pacific Northwest Leather history.

Jack says that S/M has informed his life and his personal spiritual path for more than thirty years, bringing him lifelong friendships, great enlightenment, and much joy and pleasure.

....

Kristen Knapick, MA, LMHCA, is a psychotherapist in private practice in Seattle. She specializes in working with those for whom kink/poly/sex work/queerness/gender variance are a part of life, whether the source of a problem or not. Her nearly twenty years of experience as a member of all of these communities give her a unique, non-judgmental perspective on mental health within them, and her professional training has sharpened her skills.

Kristen has presented material at Babeland, Powersurge, Living in Leather, the Center for Sex Positive Culture, Women in Kink, and Gender Odyssey. She has organized professional trainings for mental health providers on polyamory and BDSM and created a research project to explore the aging of the transgender community and the ways in which our current system is unprepared for assisting these trailblazers. Currently, Kristen is working to raise awareness and visibility for the needs of transpeople/gender-nonconformists, sex workers, and kinky and/or polyamorous people within the mental health system.

> *"If someone had told me years ago that sharing a sense of humour was so vital to partnerships, I could have avoided a lot of sex."*
>
> Kate Beckinsale

Week 4

Expert Testimony

Checking In & Workshop

Richard: Welcome, everyone!

I'm glad you've all had an opportunity to meet and greet. This process works best if we're not complete strangers to one another. And I hope the thumbnail sketches I provided you were helpful too.

(Note to the reader: Remember, the thumbnail sketches of the panelists appeared at the end of the last chapter.)

Now that we're settled, let's begin. This week, like last week, our check-in and workshop segments will be combined. Participants, you will be asking all the questions and directing the discussion. Panelists, you are welcome to comment on whatever questions you would like. And I think it's safe to assume that because of the diversity of your backgrounds, we will be hearing an array of different opinions.

Alicia, would you start us off?

Alicia: Hi everyone! I've really been looking forward to today's session. I can't believe I'm in such amazing company.

So here's my first question: I've been sensing my partner Blake's dissatisfaction with his role as a top in our BDSM play. But, until now, I didn't know what to say to him about it. I want to be more supportive of his discernment process, but I just don't know how. Any suggestions?

Kristen: You may want to take a look at how you've noticed his growing dissatisfaction. What were the clues you were picking up? Is it something about his behavior or is it just a feeling you are having? You'll want to parse that out because then you'll know what to take to him when you check in with him next time.

You could begin with something like, "I've noticed it takes you longer to get ready for play lately and I wanted to check out what might be going on." Use something like this as an intro to discussing your concerns. This open-endedness will give him room to share his thoughts with you.

Let him know that it matters to you that you're both satisfied with the play you are enjoying together. Ask him what's going on and then just listen. That's the most supportive thing you can do; give him a safe space for him to speak and then just listen.

Samantha: Does any of this dissatisfaction have to do with a particular aspect of BDSM? I mean, are there things you guys don't like? It's my experience that folks new to the scene feel as if they need to embrace the whole shebang instead of parsing through the array of available power exchange expressions to find the things that truly interest them. For example, if someone doesn't like to inflict pain then I'd suggest that person explore other ways of topping.

Folks new to the scene can also experience a bit of performance anxiety. Some feel enormous pressure to "do it right." That can cause great insecurity and that's never a good thing. Like much of sex, one learns what works and what doesn't by doing. I'm glad that you and your partner are doing a lot of hands-on learning. This will help each of you find the expressions you truly enjoy.

Of course, there's also the possibility that your partner may have simply discovered that topping isn't, or is no longer, a turn on. Period. If that is the case, then it's best that he follow his heart to his next adventure.

Byrdie: From your bio it sounds like you've already been discussing it, so that's a great start!

If the two of you attend hands-on workshops where participants are expected to bring a partner on which to practice, how often is Blake your practice bottom? Learning from an instructor can feel like bottoming, which could keep you both somewhat comfortable while learning, Alicia.

Also, if you can negotiate it, perhaps you could co-top Blake with a more experienced player. This option would keep you in the student seat while you're learning and Blake gets to practice his bottoming skills. As long as he's willing to encourage you along your topping learning curve and be patient with you, both of you could learn a different play dynamic together.

Lance: I'm always concerned about, and perhaps even critical of, people who have taken on one-sided roles in relationships; those people who claim to be exclusive tops or exclusive bottoms. I think we all need balance in our lives.

The truth of the matter is that our lives outside sex or the scene can often determine what role we choose for ourselves inside sex or the scene. For example, someone who is in control in all other aspects of their daily life may opt for a more submissive role in sex or a scene. And the opposite can also be true.

To my way of thinking, it takes being a good bottom to be a good top and vice versa.

The best thing you can do, Alicia, is to have a heart-to-heart talk with your partner, like Kristen suggested. You could begin by discussing the need for balance, both in your life as well as his. Honest communication is essential for understanding where you guys have been together and where each of you hope to go in the future. Don't be afraid of your truth. I always say we are only responsible for the hurt that comes with dishonesty, not from honesty.

After your heart-to-heart, you can implement some of the aspects of this role reversal in terms of your actual play. You might, on occasion, introduce a few aspects of the unfamiliar role for your partner. For example, if your partner is usually the top or in the dominant role, you could experiment by assuming that role yourself. Light bondage, some sensory depravation, i.e. blindfold or hood, perhaps even a gag, could be employed in an attempt to help him learn how to surrender. Then you might add some sexual arousal to the play. Your partner won't be able to reciprocate because of the bondage, so he will only be able to receive. And if your partner is someone who has always been on top, or in the dominant role, this will make for interesting new sensations. It could easily open the door for further experimentation with role reversals. And in the process, you, who have generally been the bottom or submissive, will be exercising your top/Dom muscles.

Willie: Any tips for two dominants in a relationship? And would the same advice hold true for two submissives?

Lance: The difficulty for some to give up control, as well as for some to assume control, basically comes from the same place—performance anxiety. In the first instance, it may be a question of the dominant becoming vulnerable in the submissive role. In the second instance, it may be a question of the submissive not knowing what to do in the dominant role. Both, I assume, have to do with a lack of experience in the role opposite from what they are most familiar with. That's easily dealt with through role-reversal exercises.

Let me suggest a simple communication exercise. Sit face-to-face, legs crossed on the floor with your knees touching. Hold one another's hands in front of you. Now, one at a time, tell your partner the things you love and admire about him/her. You may discover that this exercise will open the emotional floodgates between you. Two dominants doing this exercise will immediately experience the vulnerability of being on the receiving end of these disclosures. This emotional vulnerability could then be translated to sex or scene vulnerability in similar role-reversal exercises.

Getting in touch with your true feelings for one another can break up the logjam in the power dynamic of a relationship. But, unaddressed, this blockage will surely destroy a relationship.

Samantha: I have a question for you. Are you both really true dominants? Or maybe you're capable of submission, but neither one of you is willing to switch, even if it is only with one another. Either way, I've got to say that some of the best scenes I've had were ones where people couldn't tell who was the top in the scene.

I gather from what I read in your thumbnail sketches that you guys have permission to involve other people in your play. That's good because both of you can then have a lovely time dominating someone else.

And I don't see why this advice couldn't be as easily applicable for two submissives in a relationship. All they'd have to do is find a dominant to lead a scene for them both.

Stan: Could we talk a little bit about the psychology of a submissive? What role does confidence play in submissiveness?

Like how can a sub be confident without being cocky?

Byrdie: There's a wonderful article offered by Cracked.com, of all places, called "6 Harsh Truths that Will Make You a Better Person", by David Wong. The piece begins with:

"Feel free to stop reading this if your career is going great, you're thrilled with your life and you're happy with your relationships. Enjoy the rest of your day, friend, this article is not for you. You're doing a great job, we're all proud of you.

For the rest of you, I want you to try something: Name five impressive things about yourself. Write them down or just shout them out loud to the room. But here's the catch—you're not allowed to list anything you are (i.e., I'm a nice guy, I'm honest), but instead can only list things that you do (i.e., I just won a national chess tournament, I make the best chili in Massachusetts). If you found that difficult, well, this is for you, and you are going to fucking hate hearing it. My only defense is that this is what I wish somebody had said to me around 1995 or so."

Wong goes on to enumerate six things that will make you a better person. Of particular interest to you, Stan, would be #3—You Hate Yourself Because You Don't Do Anything:

"'So, what you're saying that I should pick up a book on how to get girls?' Only if step one in the book is 'Start making yourself into the type of person girls want to be around.'

Because that's the step that gets skipped—it's always 'How can I get a job?' and not 'How can I become the type of person employers want?' It's 'How can I get pretty girls to like me?' instead of 'How can I become the type of person that pretty girls like?' See, because that second one could very well require giving up many of your favorite hobbies and paying more attention to your appearance, and God knows what else. You might even have to change your personality."

The entire article is worth a read. As Wong says, "Remember, misery is comfortable. It's why so many people prefer it. Happiness takes effort."

Kristen: Submissives actually have to have a great deal of confidence in themselves, and in their Dominants, for the relationship to be sustainable. Playing with fear and power ought not interfere with confidence. As for cocky, that's just confidence that can't keep its mouth shut.

Learn to keep your mouth shut! Instead, listen for what's going on beneath the obvious.

Lance: Kristen's right! Confidence and cockiness stem from two different places. Confidence is genuine and comes without effort. It comes from a place of growth and awareness, where cockiness comes from a place of shallowness and insecurity.

In terms of the psychology of a submissive, I think I already addressed that in my response to an earlier question. A trust-bond with your Dom is essential. You must also trust yourself. Without these components there is no power exchange.

The sub that wants to control everything is not an authentic submissive. So if your preconceived ideas about what your Domme is supposed to look like, or how she should behave, or how she sets up the scene, are getting in the way of your being submissive to her, then you deserve what you will surely get—nothing. This is a red flag signaling a lack of trust, a sense of superiority, and an arrogance that is unbecoming in a submissive.

If this is happening to you, then you need to take a very close look at yourself indeed. Nothing short of reshaping the paradigm of how you interact with the world will do.

Gretchen: I want to know if any of you have thoughts on syncing up what we want in life with what we are emotionally capable of? I mean, how can we develop a skill set to showcase our capacities so we get what makes us happy?

Kristen: I do have thoughts about that. And in light of what I read about you in the thumbnail sketch Richard sent me, I want to tell you, Gretchen, that it's asking an extraordinary amount of your psyche to adapt to multiple changes on multiple levels of your primary relationship. You are already looking at moving from a part-time M/s relationship to one that is 24/7. Your kids have recently left your home. Those things alone are substantial, life-altering changes and now you and Eddie are considering a move into polyamory. I think all of this is more than is fair to ask of one person at any given time.

And may I also suggest that it is probably unfair to ask this other submissive woman, whoever she might be, to come into a situation that is still shifting.

Insofar as syncing up what you want with what you are emotionally capable of, this is the perfect time to slow down, take a deep breath, and communicate, communicate, communicate! This is a time for transparency, self-acceptance, and an opportunity to improve communication skills with your primary partner, maybe even through couple's therapy with a kink-positive therapist.

Lance: To paraphrase one of my most favorite quotes: "Our greatest fear is not that we are inadequate; our greatest fear is that we are powerful beyond measure." I personally don't think that there is anything we are emotionally incapable of. However, that doesn't mean that things will always come easily.

Setting boundaries is a sure-fire way of avoiding many of the pitfalls that come from living on the edge. Knowing what is expected of us and having a sense of security that we won't be surprised by things we aren't prepared to handle helps build self-confidence and confidence in the bond we have with our intimate partner(s).

Eddie: Kristen, thank you for including me in your response to Gretchen. I never really considered the emotional and psychological toll my desire to include a second female submissive into our family may be having on not only Gretchen, but me too. Lots to think about.

My question is about confidence in a M/s relationship. How does one best instill a sense of confidence in the one he wishes to dominate? I mean if there's no bond of trust, then the power exchange is nothing more than a power trip, right?

Byrdie: Make an effort to be sure everyone involved in the relationship understands that they're being heard. When each person feels properly honored by the others, it'll create a sense of confidence in all partners. I've found two of Gary Chapman's books, *The Five Love Languages* and *The Five Apology Languages*, helpful. I find it important to consider that even people close to me require different kinds of gestures of love and/or apology in order that they know they are indeed cherished.

Lance: This is our second question about confidence, isn't it? Stan asked about confidence in terms of the submissive role; now you, Eddie ask the same question from the dominant role.

Let's be honest, a lot of what passes as dominant behavior in the culture is actually power tripping. These kinds of tops/Doms are in it only for themselves; it's all about them. They have no real concern for their bottoms/subs. All the fun, playful elements of the scene are gone because the top/Dom is not connected or present.

Sex, as well as power exchange, is a dance. And the dance requires that both players are in sync. Otherwise they are stepping all over one another and making a muddle of the whole thing.

Kristen: Lance is right. You instill trust by knowing what you are doing physically and emotionally. Do your homework! Do the necessary research, take time to practice, and a little transparency along the way wouldn't hurt either.

Seiko: Is there such a thing as a closet sub? If there is, I think I may be one.

Kristen: I suggest that you may need some help with your internalized oppression. And the help you need must be culturally sensitive. I think what you are describing has little or nothing to do with power exchange. I gather from the thumbnail sketch I got from Richard that your sense of shame about the submissive role is a reaction to the appalling way you see Asian women depicted in the popular culture—subservient and powerless.

I suspect there may also be a bit of emotional and psychological whiplash going on. You are powerful and dominant in the workplace, but considerably less so at home in your relationship with your roommate Xiang. Am I right about that?

Seiko: You're absolutely right, Kristen. I've never experienced anything like this in my life.

Would you mind if I asked a follow-up question? Any advice for someone who may be afraid of subbing because she equates it with a sign of weakness?

Kristen: I suggest some mindfulness skill-building. This will offer you a way to become aware without becoming emotionally attached. Mindfulness exercises will offer a little objectivity.

Lance: Like Kristen mentioned earlier, I'm sensing some cultural overlay here. If your concept of subbing is bound up with subjugation and being servile, then you need to rethink this.

Consensual submission, like that practiced in power exchange, has absolutely nothing to do with the social conditioning that oppresses women around the world.

A submissive in a D/s relationship has to be strong and powerful enough to permit herself to surrender. Besides, you can be submissive in a power exchange relationship with women without ever being submissive to a man, right?

Byrdie: I took a few classes from Fetish Diva Midori and she takes issue with labels and the negative stereotypes that get built up around them. At her suggestion, I'm trying out describing my role as that of "hedonist" rather than top/bottom, Dom/sub or whatever. This new designation currently fits because I want what I want when I want it.

If you ever get a chance, I highly recommend any class Midori teaches regarding finding one's D/s archetype. She uses myth, history, and even current pop-culture heroes to help her students figure out what personas best fit them in various kink roles. Perhaps if you can match your favorite archetypes to your play you might be able to find some peace and even some comfort in the idea of submitting.

Brodie: Hi, everyone! Panelists, thank you so much for offering your thoughts and advice so generously. I really appreciate it. What a gift!

Ok, my question is this: It's clear to me that we need more than just consent to make culture-oriented things work. Do you have any suggestions or practical tools that will assist us in maintaining and deepening our kinky and BDSM relationships?

Byrdie: I'm finding that just continuing to educate myself via counseling, classes, books, and conferences is helping me a great deal. I've been able to take what

I've learned and I discuss it with others, which opens other doors.

Sofie: Ditto to what Brodie just said. You guys rock!

I have a concern that there are virtually no successful culture-oriented relationship role models in the popular culture. There are no pop stars, political figures, or athletes out there waving the freak flag. Where do you suggest we look for help in forming and maintaining kinky and BDSM relationships?

Lance: Why not be your own role model, Sofie? I mean, even if there were loads of celebrities out there waving the freak flag, you'd still have to be your own person. You can always find people to emulate, but you'll never be them. And I don't know about you, but I don't live like the rich and famous. So even if there were loads of out and proud celebrity kinksters, they would be ineffectual role models for me.

Our sexually repressed society makes it nearly impossible for celebrities to "come out," as it were. But, curiously enough, those of us without celebrity status may actually have an easier time of it. The pressure to conform is not so great on us as it is on them.

I suppose you could expend a lot of time and energy searching for a sexual guru, or you could spend that time and energy becoming your own guru.

Blake: My question is about mismatched expectations that can easily undermine a relationship. Do any of you have suggestions on how to establish an ongoing negotiation process?

Kristen: This is actually a concern for all relationships from friends, to coworkers, to family members, to lovers, to the cashier at the grocery store. So I think the only way to approach this question is in a very broad manner.

This is what check-ins are for. Whether it's me checking in with the cashier at the store—*Oh wait, I thought this was on sale?*—to me checking in with a partner at our weekly, formal check-in at the coffee shop, it's all the same thing.

Lance: Mutually agreed-upon boundaries and frequent check-ins are my suggestions.

If you can say about your partners: *I know they love me because I can talk to them and they will hear me and there's no blame,* then I think that, regardless of mismatched expectations, talking things through will strengthen your relationship, not undermine it.

I said this before, but it bears repeating: You are only responsible for the hurt that comes from being dishonest.

I also suspect that mismatched expectations that occur in culture-oriented relationships often spring from us trying to carry over a value system from our old vanilla life into our new alt life.

Byrdie: One of the things Midori says that she likes to do is curl up with a potential play partner, regardless if the partner is new to her or a longtime friend. While they are cuddling she asks them what they're craving on that particular day. This is great advice for checking in with a partner, but it's also a valuable recommendation for checking in with ourselves. *Do I want to just scream and leap all over them or do I want my partner to run a bath and pamper me until I figure out what to do with them next? Say, that bath sure sounds good.*

I think there's value in this type of self-negotiation. After all, there is generally more than one way to fulfill one's role.

Mark: People joke about topping from the bottom, but is this just a cliché? If it's not, what can be said about this? Is there any chance it could be a way for two tops to switch from time to time?

Jack: Finally, an opportunity to chime in.

Here's the thing, topping from the bottom is not a joke. It is disrespectful and insubordinate. And as a top, I will not allow it. If a bottom I am playing with attempts to top from the bottom, I will immediately stop the scene and send them home.

In my book, topping from the bottom is NOT a way for two tops to play together.

Kristen: I agree with Jack, topping from the bottom is not just a cliché; it's a reality. I prefer to call it what it really is: passive-aggressive manipulation. That's what's actually happening. And the only way this is a useful tool is if both parties have a fetish for passive-aggressive manipulation. Otherwise it simply reflects poor communication.

Lance: I don't know, maybe we need a bit of a clarification about what we are talking about here. If we are talking about the top being the only one in control, while the bottom is simply there to receive what is being meted out, then that's not what power exchange means to me.

For me, a bottom's needs are just as important as a top's needs. For me, the bottom sets the agenda, at least in terms of intensity and degree. I mean that's what the negotiation process is all about, right?

If, for some reason, you're skipping over this essential element of power play, then where's the mutuality? And if the bottom isn't being fulfilled in the scene because there were no negotiations, or less than adequate negotiations, and the bottom tries to remedy that by making demands during the scene, well, that's not a joke, that's a fuckin' shame.

Authentic power exchange is a collaborative effort. The top is the bottom and the bottom is the top. I believe the bottom should be active in his/her role as much as the top needs to be receptive in her/his role.

However, if the bottom is trying to control everything because there is no trust-bond with his/her top, well then there is nothing submissive about that. It also suggests to me that the bottom doesn't much trust him/herself either.

Samantha: I've always had mixed feelings about this phrase because, as Lance suggests, we may not always be talking about the same thing. For example, I've been known to bottom for a novice top and, generally speaking, it's a lot of fun. Of course, more often than not, those occasions were opportunities for the novice top to get some experience with a new skill.

Then there are those bottoms that know what they want and how they want it. Good for them! I suppose if they were being THAT specific about what they want with the wrong top, there'd be hell to pay. But for a top who is less of a rigorist, the accommodation could easily work out for all concerned.

Consider for a moment the top who enjoys being flogged. When I've seen this sort of thing in the past it was perfectly clear to me that the top, who just so happened to be receiving the flogging, was also the one running the scene. I mean really, as long as the people involved in the scene are having a good time, who cares what an outside observer might think?

Alicia: I prefer to keep my emotional relationships and my play relationships separate. My power-exchange play is rarely about sex, at least not in terms of it being directed toward orgasm. I've been hearing much the same thing from others in the scene lately. I wonder, is this a trend?

Kristen: Who cares if it's a trend? What works for you is what works for you. What the rest of us do is immaterial.

Byrdie: Wow, Alicia. We could make an entire workshop out of trying to answer your question. There are so many possible things to consider.

- **Play relationships**: sex play, topping, and bottoming
- **Power exchange relationships**: dominance, submission, mastery, ownership, and slavery
- **Emotional relationships**: friendships, dating partners, polyamory, lovers, partners, and spouses

I've met people who can keep all these things compartmentalized enough so that there's little, if any, overlap. I also know Masters who are married to their slaves, bottoms who fall into subspace while playing, and any other number of configurations.

Ever since I started reading up on the topic of BDSM, there's been a vocal group of people who insist that there is no place for an emotional connection between any players, and that they themselves would avoid it. I also know a fair number of people who will not combine sex with their kink unless they're in a committed relationship with said play partner or not at all.

I don't think it's a new trend, but I do see it as an established path.

Blake: What resources are available for me to learn about things like structure, protocols, standing orders, service, rituals, and Leather history?

Jack: I did not learn about these things from books or classes. I am sure there are such classes available, but I haven't a clue as to where to send you to find them.

I am in my sixties and was raised by my two grandmothers and my great-grandmother, all born before the turn of the twentieth century. And while they may roll in their coffins to think that I have taken what they taught me and applied it to sadomasochism, I am pleased and proud to think that some of their human kindness, personal codes of conduct, and impeccable manners have rubbed off on me.

Byrdie: They probably did, Jack. The image of them teaching you kink etiquette is going to keep me smiling for a while.

Depending on your local scene and how far you're willing to travel, there's a fair amount out there:

- **Conferences**: I'm not sure that there are kinky conferences on every continent, but in the western world there are plenty. I believe that every region and time zone in the US has them, and that most major cities host at least one a year.
- **Retreats**: Midori's Forte Femme intensive, Southwest Leather's Butchmann's Experience, and various retreats for submissives and slaves exist.
- **Books**: Nazca Plains Books, Iron Rose, Cleiss Press, and Down There Press all publish books on kink, and if your local bookstores don't carry them, then check with your favorite online retailer.
- **Workshops**: Local kink groups, retailers, and large kink events host classes, workshops, lectures, and demonstrations.
- **Online courses**: Some educators of note have their own websites. And there are services like Kink Academy that offer video classes taught by a variety of folks.

Sofie: I have a poly question or six. I know that both space and togetherness are important. But is there such a thing as too much of one and not enough of the other?

Kristen: I think that's a subjective thing. I think the ratio of one to the other needs to be satisfactory for all concerned. In other words, your mileage will vary.

<Laughter>

Seriously, whatever that ratio is for you, that's your normal. It's not only ok, but it's your job to make sure that you maintain the balance that keeps you feeling healthy.

And if you find that you are not living up to the expectations of one or another of your partners, then it's high time to have a conversation about expectations and boundaries. Other people's expectations of you are not your responsibility, but addressing them is!

Byrdie: I agree with Kristen. There definitely is such a thing as too much of one and not enough of the other. And finding just the right mixture varies from person to person.

The most obvious example of this is on the introversion/extroversion scale, but life history, mental, and emotional health issues, and daily stress levels can also affect how much space and togetherness you might need at any particular time.

Lance: I have to split my time between two boyfriends. I try to keep that as equitable as possible, but there are always complications. Checking in with each of my partners, from time to time, is important in maintaining that balance. And equally important is being aware of my own needs. I continually have to ask myself, *Have I been getting enough at-home time? Am I getting enough of me-time? Am I feeling overwhelmed?*

If you're feeling the need to be around people just so that you feel complete, then that's a sure sign that you're not taking care of yourself properly.

Sofie: I have a follow-up question, if I could. How does one avoid being swallowed up by one's partner(s)?

Kristen: One word: boundaries.

Lance: Love, respect, and consideration for oneself and one's partners. If that's not paramount in your poly relationships, you will be swallowed up.

If one or another of your partners is unhappy or unsupportive of what's going on with you or your other relationships, that can't be ignored. The toxicity of this unresolved discord will affect everyone concerned. Your partners need not love one another as you love them, but your partners must respect one another as the objects of your love. I'm not talking about just tolerating one another; I'm talking about real respect, support, and ultimately affirmation.

Byrdie: A favorite piece of advice along these lines is to consider your relationship with yourself to be your *primary* relationship. This is the relationship that takes precedence over all others. Spend time building that relationship—figuring out self-care, self-rescue, and other regular forms of self-love—so that when you add another partner to the mix you won't be consumed by the other, even if that partner is your "primary" partner.

Healthy relationships involve upholding all of your agreements with your partner(s), barring accidents and emergencies. If you wouldn't consider disappointing a partner, then you should really think twice before disappointing your most important partner: yourself.

Eddie: Kristen, I know you touched on this earlier in responding to Gretchen, but I thought, since this is such an important issue for me, I'd ask point-blank. Do any of you have suggestions for bringing in a new sub into an established, long-term, exclusive M/s or D/s relationship?

Lance: I suspect that even under the best of circumstances, this is not an easy thing to do. I sense that it's not all that different from a couple adopting a child into an already established family. First thing, you have to make sure there's total mutual interest.

I know a gay male couple that is considering this. The adoption is the heart's desire of one of the men, but his partner is more like, *Ok, I guess. I'll do it for you.* That's just not going to work. I know other male couples that have considered adopting a "boy" or "pup," and I'm talking in scene terms here, in an effort to revitalize or strengthen a shaky relationship. That's never a good decision.

It's never good to bring someone new into an ailing situation in the hopes that the new person will be the remedy for what's broken in the primary relationship.

My advice, Eddie, is to check in with Gretchen and try to discover why either one or both of you want to attempt this life-altering feat. If you discover that it is for strictly selfish reasons, don't move forward.

Begin by evaluating your intentions. Check to make sure that both individuals in the couple are equally committed to this alteration. And as far as I'm concerned, if the Master is doing this unilaterally, despite the concerns of his/her slave, than that's a misuse of the power exchange. Then take your time with the implementation. You simply can't rush something like this.

Rely on this adage: *When the teacher is ready the student will appear.* If you have to go looking for this addition, then I'm going to guess you're rushing the process.

Jack: I have a less benign perspective on this.

Eddie, what you propose is dangerous and fraught with pitfalls because you are deliberately unbalancing what already has been carefully balanced. I suggest that you ask yourself why you feel compelled to do this. It's my experience that we can and often do lie to ourselves about why we have to do something like this. And despite this, we do it anyway because we are compelled to take that risk.

Eddie: Thank you for being so honest with me. So let me ask a follow-up question. Do any of you have tips on how to build dynamic and healthy communication habits into our alt relationships?

Kristen: If you don't already know the basics of nonviolent communication, this is the time to learn. Because, as we all know, it's not only what we say, it's how we say it.

Lance: The biggest impediment to building dynamic and healthy communication habits into a relationship are those difficult messages that we have to relate to our partner from time to time. If it were just a matter of communicating all the happy, good stuff, I suspect none of us would have a problem with our communication habits. So for those times when we are confounded by what to do with those difficult messages, let me turn you onto a technique that works very well for me. It's called a compliment sandwich: compliment—criticism—compliment. Tell your partner something you really like about her/him, tell your partner the thing that gets on your nerves, tell your partner another thing that you really like about him/her.

Richard: That reminds me of that old joke about the troubled couple in therapy. The therapist suggests this very same compliment sandwich exercise to the couple and then invites the husband to begin. He says; "I like what you are doing with your hair. You're a bitch! Nice shoes."

<Laughter>

Sorry, I just couldn't resist.

On that note, I think it's time for us to take a short break. Stretch your legs, grab some refreshments, and we'll regroup in fifteen minutes.

My Check-In

Richard: What questions did you prepare for today's session? Have any of them been addressed by our panelists yet? Did our discussion so far raise any new questions for you? Would you like to respond to any of the questions or concerns raised by your fellow participants? Would you like to respond to any of the comments made by of our panelists?

Richard: All settled in once again? Good! Let's resume. Do you have another question, Seiko?

Seiko: Yes, I do.

This is a real tender subject for me, but I need help with this, so here goes. I'm having difficulty coming to grips with the affection I have for my female roommate and sometime play partner, Xiang. I've always been straight and now I feel so lost and confused. Can anyone help me?

Lance: I have a couple of questions before I comment. Do your affections for your roommate contain a sexual component? And, if so, are these sexual feelings associated solely with her?

If you answered *yes* to either or both of these questions, you will want to tread lightly. I suggest that before you disturb the relationship equilibrium you have with your roommate, you might want to begin playing with a few other women. And by play, I mean scene play. This experimentation will allow you the opportunity to see if your attraction is indeed specific to Xiang. You may discover that, thanks to your roommate, your eroticism is expanding to include women in general. And if that's the case, you'll have a whole lot more information about yourself if/when you choose to come out, as it were, to your Xiang.

Samantha: Ya know, Seiko, not all scenes involve sex, and just because some play doesn't involve sex, doesn't mean that there isn't a bond of affection between the players.

I also think a person can express their affection for someone in a multitude of different ways. In the end, I just can't see where attraction is a genital issue. I mean, how we feel about someone has way more to do with who the other person is rather than with what resides between their legs, right? I know that's how it works for me and just look how fabulous I am!

<Laughter>

Blake: I love it! I want to be just like you, Samantha, when I grow up!

I'm wondering if any of you have experienced an awakening in terms of scene roles at any point in your life? Or do you think most people recognize who and what they are from the get-go?

Lance: For many of us, the changes we experience in life often translate into alterations in our scene roles. As our lives change, so do our needs and wants. How could that not impact how we play?

Byrdie: I certainly have experienced an awakening. I've tried on a few roles during my time in the Seattle scene, and am thankful that I paid attention when the word "hedonist" came to my attention multiple times last year. I like variety, but even the label "switch" has connotations that I'm not interested in associating myself with right now. A different label might fit me later, but "hedonist" seems very comfortable to me right now.

Blake: That's kind of what I was thinking. It just seems to me that if one settles on all of this early in life, there's no room for growth or development later on in life. Maybe one or another of you could talk about this.

Kristen: I believe that there is nothing about us that circumstances won't affect. And as circumstances change throughout our lifetime, we sometimes find it necessary to adapt our roles.

Gretchen, may I use you as an example here? It's pretty clear that you are a dyed-in-the-wool sub, right? But you're a slave to Eddie, no one else, right? I guess one would have to ask, if Eddie does indeed introduce another submissive woman to your household, what will your role-connection be to this other woman, if any?

You see, with the change in circumstance comes an opportunity to change and adapt one's role.

My take on all of this is that settling into a role is a choice. Often that choice is made out of habit, but it's still a choice. In the end, we are all free to reevaluate, grow, and develop our roles so that they better suit who we are becoming. Unfortunately, not everyone is aware or conscious of the toll that changing circumstances are taking on settled and established roles. And that's where pain comes in. It usually takes us being in emotional pain for us to recognize that it's time for a change.

Byrdie: I notice that many people have a default role or public persona that seems to fit them perfectly, except for one or two exceptions. Some of these people may have one person for whom they'd switch in either direction or behave in a certain way that would be perceived as only associated with a certain role. Our example person's role is not one of them.

There's a well-known dominant sadist in our community who actually identifies as a switch, but he never bottoms publicly because he would lose play partners if he did. He's attended discussion groups for switches and actively disturbed people just by embracing that role.

I've met sadistic submissives, service tops, indulgent Daddies; some people swap out the label, others keep their preferred label and let other people learn to cope. It really seems to depend on the person.

Brodie: We've discussed the difference between dominance and being domineering. I was having trouble with that when I was just starting out. I wonder, is this just a guy thing, or do novice fem-Dommes get called on this too?

Kristen: I say it's not a gender thing; it's a privilege thing. It can be a class thing too. But most importantly it's a personality thing. Dominance comes from a place of self-acceptance; domineering comes from fear.

Byrdie: Yes, they do get called on it too.

I think that part of it is an issue of mismatched expectations and not defining terms. I can think of a few different situations where people have stated that they take on a certain role—like "Dominant" or "submissive," carried on as they'd wanted to, and then discovered that they weren't compatible with their partners after all. Some people find that they only feel submissive while actively bottoming. Some folks don't realize that in some regions of the country, people use terms like "submissive" and "bottom" interchangeably, while others see a "submissive" as someone who devotes a certain portion of their time in service to another and see a "bottom" as someone who receives sensation from a top.

What type of X are you? When you consider that, what do you envision yourself doing? Some people may roll their eyes at the idea of having to ask oneself this sort of question, but I believe that it could save players many hours of frustration.

Willie: Do you suppose scene roles flow from our personality type? Or could they be a way of escaping the confines of our personality type?

Samantha: Yes to both.

Personally, my scenes are usually a direct reflection of my personality. I feel they are a way to express what I am feeling in the moment. I've enjoyed both very high-energy and very mellow, low-key scenes. It all comes from how I'm feeling and the chemistry I have with the person I'm playing with.

Lance: I agree with Samantha. Yes! And yes!

As I was saying earlier, our lives outside sex or a scene can often determine what role we choose for ourselves inside sex or a scene. For example, someone who is in control in all other aspects of his/her daily life may opt for a more submissive role in sex or a scene. But the opposite can also be true.

The real subversive issue here is stagnation. We often get so comfortable in our chosen or designated roles that all of the juice of the sex or a scene is drained away. I mean, where is the edginess in only playing in our comfort zone?

Playing contrary to our personality types may be just the thing needed to escape the confines of that role. Change makes us vulnerable and opens the door to experimentation that can free us up from the usual or the expected.

Jack: If you can escape the confines of your "personality type," then, in my opinion, your "personality type" is much bigger than you think it is, or is much bigger than you will admit.

We have the roles that we let others see, and the roles that we keep hidden from some or all others, but all of these roles are still ours. They are all a part of our whole self and sit together in the circle that is "oneself."

Brodie: Do you suppose the skills we learn in BDSM, the ones that teach us how to deal with uncomfortable and stressful situations, can be equally applicable in our day-to-day life and in our relationship building? Do you have any examples of this from your own life?

Byrdie: After being part of a community where asking before touching someone is expected and normal behavior, I've found negotiating casual touch with people I'm not currently intimate with fascinating. Many balk at the very idea of having to ask me first and accuse me of being touch-negative. It's particularly galling when, after I explain to them why I want them to ask for my permission, they continue to insist that I don't like to be touched. Apparently they don't hear the part that specifies "without my prior consent." These people seem to have a hard time functioning socially without feeling entitled to touch my body however they wish.

I think that part of this comes from the propaganda some in the touchy-feely crowd have heard about initiating touch. I'm lookin' at you, Leo Buscaglia. When they encounter someone like me who has absorbed equally comforting propaganda from a different perspective, they seem to experience a bit of cognitive dissonance.

Some eventually come around, perhaps after doing their own separate research on the topic, but many still seem actively disturbed by having their default behavior questioned.

Lance: It's a general life lesson to never become too comfortable with who we are. I think it's good for us to keep stretching our boundaries.

Fear can be a strong motivator. Some fear is good because it keeps us out of harm's way, but a lot of the things we are afraid of stem from our insecurities. This kind of fear is just holding us back from doing the things that would enable us to grow.

What we learn in BDSM is how to confront and move through our fears—the fear of submission, the fear of control, or the fear of receiving without needing to reciprocate. So yes, I think the skills we learn in our culture-related lives can indeed positively impact our day-to-day lives.

Kristen: I totally agree! Absolutely, they're applicable. The communication skills we learn in kink are not exclusive to BDSM. In fact, they are precisely the same communication skills all people in relationships need to know. However, our communication skill set has the extra layer of power exchange and physical safety concerns added to it.

I apply the skills I've learned in scene negotiation—*This is what I want, this is why I want it, and this is why you should give it to me; now let's negotiate*—in my everyday involvement with people, like getting what I want from a sales clerk, car mechanic, or waiter, and it works.

Sofie: Can a person turn this kinky stuff on and off like I seem to be able to do? Is that even healthy?

Byrdie: Listen, if this kinky stuff, as you call it, supports the life you want to lead, it's healthy. But if it's causing a problem, then it's not. Many people compartmentalize their lives, take breaks from the scene, and so on. So there's nothing unusual about that.

Sofie: Ok, so let me ask you this. I suppose if we hang out in the culture long enough we're bound to meet folks who are making things work, but that's a big If for a lot of us. Most of us, myself included, have to keep our alt identities under wraps, and hiding creates its own problems. Any thoughts on how we can live authentically while still being circumspect about revealing who we are?

Kristen: Fantastic question! But let me rephrase slightly. My question would be: How do we live with integrity and authenticity but still maintain a comfortable level of privacy? You see the difference between your question and mine? It's privacy vs. secrecy. Secrets beget shame; privacy begets boundaries.

We begin this process of discernment with taking stock of our core values and then making decisions about how we interact with the world in such a way that we remain in alignment with those core values. This allows for optimum peace of mind with our identities, regardless of the pressures to identify as one thing or another. This is no one's business but yours.

Lance: I believe that coming out is important.

To bring us back to one of your previous questions, you don't have to wave your freak flag all over the place, but being honest about who you are with those people who are important in your life is, I think, necessary. The only way to educate the world is by being honest with the world. There's nothing enlightened about shrinking ourselves so that those around us will feel secure. When you allow your light to shine you give the people around you the permission to do the same.

This is how I feel about coming out as a sex worker. It's my way of letting people know that not all sex workers hate their work. There is nothing that is inherently degrading or negative about my work. And once I explain this, I shift their paradigm. They may not embrace sex work as I do, but I certainly make them think.

Byrdie: There are plenty of people who use scene names and keep their faces out of photographs, etc.

I know of one woman who'd been very active in the local scene. She was a schoolteacher and insisted on discretion lest she be persecuted out of her career. She set a goal for herself and kept it: She charted when her earliest students would be legally old enough to join the kink community, and then dropped out of public kink life the night before. We miss seeing her around, but to my mind her logic was flawless. She continues to work in education and now only plays privately.

Eddie: How does a couple slip out of their 24/7 M/s or D/s roles to engage in important relationship discussions?

Kristen: Thank you for that question because this is really important. I suggest regularly scheduled check-ins. And it must be assumed and agreed on that both parties have equal power during these formal discussions. Roles need to be put aside, at least temporarily, to discuss practical relationship issues.

I think what this question is pointing to is: How do we do this in a significant and meaningful way as well as make it different from the rest of our lives? And that feels like ritual to me.

I think we create ritual that is reserved for this leveling of power. It could be anything from removing a collar or a piece of jewelry that is meant to signify the formal power exchange. And when the meeting is over, it goes back on.

If nothing like that exists, then you should set up these meetings in a neutral place outside of your power exchange dynamic, like a coffeehouse.

In this instance, both parties would meet at an arranged time and place, but each would arrive separately. You have your meeting, conduct your business, and leave separately. The 24/7 relationship resumes once you are back together. So in other words, you are bracketing off these encounters from your everyday life.

One of the things that makes this kind of communication so delicate is that the environment must be safe for all involved. The Master or top in this situation needs to "take a step back" in order to make room for the sub or bottom to "take a step forward" for the duration.

Lance: To my mind, roles are roles; they are not rules. If your roles are carved in stone, I suspect that your relationship will be equally rigid. And that kind of rigidity doesn't allow for much growth, if any.

Jack: I take a significantly different view of this. If it is truly a 24/7 M/s or D/s relationship, they cannot "slip out of it" without redefining it. You cannot have it both ways. If a relationship is truly a 24/7 M/s or D/s relationship, the responsibilities of each party are clearly defined. You don't enter into such a relationship without thinking long and hard about all possible contingencies. 24/7 M/s or D/s relationships ought not to be entered into lightly.

Stan: Any tips on connecting with and/or attracting a dominant woman?

Kristen: The best tip I can offer you, my friend, is get some therapy. Clearly you have a great deal of oppression going on. Therapy, with a kink-positive therapist, will help you confront and accept your identity. And until you do this you have absolutely no business engaging in the scene.

Byrdie: I know I'm beginning to sound like the reference librarian, but I recommend an article on the Kink in Exile site (kinkinexile.wordpress.com) from way back in 2009. It is titled "What Do Dominant Women Want?" Be sure to go back and read the whole article because I'm only going to list the authors' (kinkinexile and Iron Rose) thoughts.

1. The small stuff does matter. It tells me that he is attracted to

me because I'm me, not just any dominant woman.

2. He makes it clear how important I am to him. He makes room in his schedule for me. He does little things to show me that he's been thinking about me when we aren't together, like writing me letters or buying me little gifts.

3. I don't have to wonder if he wants to be here. He says please and thank you. He is clear and honest on his boundaries.

4. He does not confuse the fantasy of submission with the reality of submission. He has a life, a career, friends, and hobbies. He is a person, with a personality outside of being a submissive.

5. When he serves me he actually serves *me* rather than his own fantasies. If he runs errands for me, he does it right, and to the best of his abilities. He doesn't offer to run errands for me just to get my attention, and he doesn't mess up on purpose to make me "punish" him.

6. I am not his dirty little secret. Nor is kink his dirty little secret. He should not be ashamed of his submission.

7. He understands that I have many facets. He does not suddenly lose the ability to bottom to me because I bottomed to someone else.

8. His submission is personally meaningful. He does not think that being a submissive means being someone other than who he is. I want the submission to be personally meaningful, not just a rote framework copied from porn.

Another noteworthy article, "How To Date A Dominant Woman 101", appears on the Lipstick and Ligature blog (lipstickandligature.tumblr.com). There are ten tips, but these seem to be the most relevant to your question:

1. Ignore EVERYTHING you have ever seen in porn.

3. Find out what other stuff she is interested in. Remember, when she's not tying you up/beating you, you will need to fill the silence with actual conversations about stuff.

7. Be courteous, polite, and mindful that she's not your mother.

8. Make sure she's comfortable and happy and feels safe and loved.

9. Submissive men, particularly young men, can make the mistake of confusing arrogant, demanding and emotionally manipulative women with sexual dominance. (Women can do this too in mistaking emotionally weak and insecure men as submissive. I speak from experience.) Respect yourself and respect your lady; make your submission and her dominance emotionally significant. Find someone who loves you as much as you care for them.

Lance: Many men who fail at attracting the dominant woman of their dreams do so because they have porn-induced images of what a Domme is supposed to look like and how she is supposed to behave. If you are one of these men, you have to jettison that shit immediately. Remember, what energy you put out there is the energy that you will attract. If you're not putting out positive energy that reflects your openness and receptivity to being dominated, then you won't attract anything that even remotely resembles what you seek.

Brodie: Any tips on how to come out as kinky to a potential partner that may or may not be kinky? Do you suppose this is a first date kind of discussion?

Kristen: My tip is to practice integrity. Don't pull any punches. Be clear about what you want from the beginning, and then respect your own boundaries. A potential partner doesn't need to respect your "wanting to be kinky" boundaries, but you do. If you're clear, then the rest will take care of itself. If you tell a potential partner precisely what it is you are after, your potential partner can make an informed decision about what to do with that information.

Lance: Let me ask you this. Is acceptance of, and perhaps even involvement in, your kinky life mandatory for each and every potential partner? If it is, then you should be upfront with any potential partner from the get-go. In fact, this wouldn't only be a first-date discussion, but would also have to be part of any online profile you have. This will help short-circuit future misunderstandings and misgivings.

However, if you're involved in dating just to get laid, and if getting laid doesn't have to have any kinky overtones, then maybe this discussion could be suspended till there's evidence that this partner is more than a casual hookup.

But you have to be man enough to know the difference. If you let someone become enthralled with you without knowing your full story, then that's being deceptive as well as being unfair.

Byrdie: I suggest easing a potential partner into it by perhaps suggesting a certain activity and explaining as you make your suggestion that you'd love for them to try it with you. It could be a bonding moment just like on Oprah.

<Laughter>

However, be prepared to connect what you know about this person with what benefits you think they'd get out of experimenting with you. It'll be just like selling the concept, right? And if this is truly your passion, that sell-job shouldn't be all that difficult.

I'd also like to recommend a book, *When Someone You Love is Kinky*, by Catherine Lidst and Dossie Easton. It would make an ideal gift for a potential partner who is unfamiliar with the scene.

My Turn

Richard: How did the questions you prepared for today's session compare with those asked by your fellow participants? Are any of your questions or concerns still unanswered? If they are, would you know how to find the answers on your own? Were our panelist's comments helpful to you? Did any of our discussion so far raise new questions for you? Would you like to respond to any of the questions or concerns raised so far by your fellow participants? Would you like to respond to any of the comments made by of our panelists?

Richard: Outstanding! And with that, my friends, we need to call it a day.

But before we close, I want to thank all of you for your contributions. You've made this workshop excel.

Jack, Samantha, Lance, Kristen, and Byrdie, you've outdone yourselves. We're all deeply grateful to have had so much of you. Your selflessness and kindness are only matched by your thoughtfulness and the care you have for those of us who share this amazing culture with you.

Alicia and Blake, Brodie, Mark and Willie, Sofie, Gretchen and Eddie, Seiko, and Stan, I hope the last four weeks have served you well. It's been an honor and a pleasure to have spent these four weeks with you as you made this journey of discovery. It was exciting to watch you challenge yourselves and grow.

I am grateful for the friendships formed and the wisdom shared. And of course you know that I expect great things from you in the future. I trust that, when it's your turn to give back to the community what you so generously received here, you will do so willingly and make us all proud. I hope you'll take every opportunity to share what you've learned here with all those who might benefit. Hey, maybe one or another of you will want to sit on a panel for a future workshop.

Till we meet again, be well, be happy, be kind, be authentic, and be outrageous. Continue to share the good news of who you are with others, for you are indeed the embodiment of the Gospel of Kink.

About the Contributors

Samantha is a bisexual switch who has been a part of the SM and swinger communities for twelve years. Her favorite motto, which she uses for both worlds, is "If it isn't fun, then why the fuck do it?"

Following in a tradition of her own creation, she would never claim to know the One True Way. And she would not spend much time (let alone play) with anyone who would say such things.

She is an active volunteer and she has several causes (kinky and not) that she supports.

....

Lance Navarro is a performer in gay porn. Over the course of his porn career, he has been cast in many different roles primarily as a fisting bottom, but has also done sounding (urethral play), bondage (primarily as a sub), and played the Dom role in a few scenes as well.

He is also a masseur and sex worker.

He is polyamorous with two male partners. They all live in San Francisco, but live separately from each other.

His kink interests tend to come out more in his work, both with clients and in porn. He finds bondage and sensory deprivation to be especially useful with some of his clients. He also has a few clients that are into fisting and sounding. He is as skilled as a top and teacher as he is as a bottom. Spanking and flogging also interest him.

Lance is not currently active in any fetish clubs or organizations, although he regularly participates in various events and workshops.

He is a leather titleholder (Mr. Bolt Sacramento 2011) and competed at the International Mr. Leather Contest in Chicago. He is a frequent volunteer at St. James Infirmary, a clinic in San Francisco for current and former sex workers. It provides testing, counseling, and other services.

He also is a rider in the AIDS Lifecycle, a seven-day, 545-mile bike ride from SF to LA. He and has been for the last five years.

....

Byrdie is currently a student who is trying to find ways to recover from codependency in every aspect of her life including romantic relationships, friendships, and work. She says she is learning to tell the difference between her instincts and knee-jerk reactions to triggers. She's also learning not to be so afraid of failure. As she says, she has just as much right to ask for things, speak out, act, and follow her dreams as anyone else.

Years ago, and despite her explicitly stated lack of interest in BDSM, friends persuaded her to experiment. This led to her first flogging, which she says she found both odd and pleasant.

Byrdie now says she is a hedonist. She wants what she wants when she wants it. She prefers primal play (punching, biting, scratching, growling) and deep thud sensations. And she has a fondness for Daddy/girl play.

She identifies as someplace between bisexual, pansexual, and heteroflexible, and is working to improve trust and sensual intimacy with other women.

She is one of the earliest members of the Wet Spot, now the Center for Sex Positive Culture. She is an avid attendee at culture-oriented workshops and is easing back into the social scene.

A four-year kink relationship that had D/s elements was the inspiration for her undergoing therapy to recover from codependence.

Most recently Byrdie initiated the Seattle edition of Mollena Williams' *Know Your Negro,* a photography project intended to bring attention to the dearth of brown faces in the kink/Leather world.

....

Jack Slash, aka Jack the Journeyman, has been a member of the Seattle Leather community since 1982, and a practitioner of S/M since 1974. Before the year 2002, he was known as Dragon Xcalibur.

He holds two past Leather titles: Seattle Leatherwoman 1988 and Seattle Leather Ambassador 1997. In the eighties and nineties, he was a member of the now-disbanded Leather doo-wop singing group, the Sluts from Hell.

He teaches workshops, judges local and international contests on the West Coast, participates in local fund-raisers, and has led spirituality circles at Queer Leather events since the 1980s in Seattle, Portland, Vancouver, B.C., and San Francisco. Workshop presentations include blood sports, branding, impact play, fear and terror, ritual sacrifice, and honeybees.

He is a sought-after speaker on the topic of S/M and gender fluidity within the Leather community. As part of a group of community elders, he often shares his perspective on Pacific Northwest Leather history.

Jack says that S/M has informed his life and his personal spiritual path for more than thirty years, bringing him lifelong friendships, great enlightenment, and much joy and pleasure.

....

Kristen Knapick, MA, LMHCA, is a psychotherapist in private practice in Seattle. She specializes in working with those for whom kink/poly/sex work/queerness/gender variance are a part of life, whether the source of a problem or not. Her nearly twenty years of experience as a member of all of these communities give her a unique, non-judgmental perspective on mental health within them, and her professional training has sharpened her skills.

Kristen has presented material at Babeland, Powersurge, Living in Leather, the Center for Sex Positive Culture, Women in Kink, and Gender Odyssey. She has organized professional trainings for mental health providers on polyamory and BDSM, and created a research project to explore the aging of the transgender community and the ways in which our current system is unprepared for assisting these trailblazers. Currently, Kristen is working to raise awareness and visibility for the needs of transpeople/gender-nonconformists, sex workers, and kinky and/or polyamorous people within the mental health system.

About the Author

Richard Wagner, Ph.D., ACS

Richard Wagner, M.Div., Ph.D., ACS, is a psychotherapist and clinical sexologist in private practice in Seattle.

Richard has been a practitioner of sex therapy and relationship counseling for over thirty years.

He has also been involved in all sorts of sex-education and sexual-enrichment projects. One such outlet is his online sex advice column, which he's been writing for well over fifteen years. During that time it's been syndicated on a number of sites. Now his column and weekly podcasts have a home of their own: drdicksexadvice.com. He also contributes to several other websites as a guest columnist.

He is renowned for his long- and short-term seminars and workshops for healing and helping professionals, sexual minorities, men living with and through prostate cancer, and women and men affected by sex abuse and sexual trauma.

He often speaks in the public forum on policy issues related to religion, human sexuality, aging, death and dying, and the clergy sex-abuse scandal. He is a highly sought-after keynote speaker and presenter at conventions and symposia.

www.ingramcontent.com/pod-product-compliance
Lightning Source LLC
Chambersburg PA
CBHW081415270326
41931CB00015B/3287
* 9 7 8 1 6 1 0 9 8 3 6 4 8 *